trotman

REAL LIFE ISSUES:
SEX &
RELATIONSHIPS

Adele Cherreson Cole

To Mum and Papa

Real Life Issues: Sex and Relationships
This first edition published in 2004 by Trotman and Company Ltd
2 The Green, Richmond, Surrey TW9 1PL

© Trotman and Company Limited 2004

Editorial and Publishing Team
Author Adele Cherreson Cole
Editorial Mina Patria, Editorial Director; Rachel Lockhart, Commissioning Editor;
Anya Wilson, Managing Editor; Bianca Knights, Assistant Editor
Production Ken Ruskin, Head of Pre-press and Production;
James Rudge, Production Artworker
Sales and Marketing Deborah Jones, Head of Sales and Marketing
Advertising Tom Lee, Commercial Director
Managing Director Toby Trotman

Designed by XAB

British Library Cataloguing in Publication Data
A catalogue record for this book is available from the British Library

ISBN 0 85660 991 9

Typeset by Tradespools Publishing Solutions
Printed and bound in Great Britain by
Cromwell Press, Trowbridge, Wiltshire

CONTENTS:

'What's important in a relationship? Openness, intimacy, respect and friendship. Mad passionate love is great, but it doesn't last long and it's not everything.'

Shakira, 19

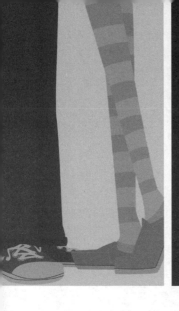

REAL LIFE ISSUES:
Sex &
Relationships

ABOUT THE AUTHOR

Adele Cherreson Cole began her writing career in 1979 on the *New Musical Express (NME)*. She went on to edit the young women's magazine *Look Now* and to work in a senior editorial role on *Cosmopolitan* in the 1980s. As a journalist and stylist she contributed to national newspapers, consumer magazines and specialist publications, writing on sex, relationships, health, beauty, fashion, interior design and travel, as well as news.

Since moving from London in the early 1990s she has managed a team of editors in a publishing company, lectured in journalism and media studies, and has extended her writing experience to include promotional material, websites, videos, presentations and books.

Adele spent five years in corporate communications at BNFL's (British Nuclear Fuel's) power generation head office and latterly worked in public relations and marketing. She now returns to her first love – writing.

Adele lives in Gloucestershire with her husband and daughter.

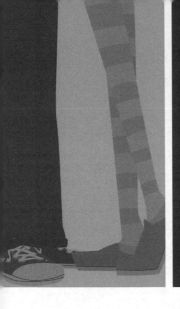

REAL LIFE ISSUES:
Sex &
Relationships

ACKNOWLEDGEMENTS

Thanks to everyone who participated in the research of this book, especially Paula Hall, Sexual & Relationship Psychotherapist and Young People's Counsellor, Relate and Christine Lacy, Senior Practice Consultant, Relate, as well as the fpa.

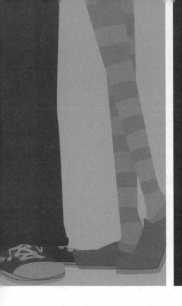

INTRODUCTION

Relationships are important to humans, whatever age, whatever nationality, whichever sex. Without relationships, life is empty, boring and lonely. With relationships, life is fun, fulfilling – and sometimes stressful. Relationships are rewarding, but a struggle too. If you're a teenager going through highs and lows, self-doubt and confusion, relationships can be a headache.

This book gives you ideas on how to manage explosive, embarrassing and scary situations with those you love, like, and fancy like mad. As well as tips and advice on handling family, friends and boyfriends/girlfriends, you'll find basic information on how to have an enjoyable and healthy sex life.

The sex bit may sound like the most interesting part, but if you're going through hormonal hell, look at the first few chapters to get a handle on how you act, why you react and how to act in your own interests.

Sex is a whole new can of worms and unless you've got friendships, home life and school or work sorted, it can add more stress, just when you don't need it. Chapters 1–5 may help you sort out your relationships.

Get sex sussed (see Chapter 6 onwards) before you do anything and you'll have more confidence and more fun. Being a sexpert (see Chapter 7) isn't just sensible, it's cool too. Even if you're years away from your first sexual encounter, gen up on the facts and be prepared to have good quality experiences when you're ready to take it further.

This book gives 13–19 year olds solid information, sound advice and terrific tips on surviving the stresses of sex and relationships as a teenager. It's part of the Real Life Issues series to help teenagers overcome some of the difficulties of growing up and getting on. If you have other issues or problems, look out for books in the series on: Addictions, Bullying, Confidence and Self-Esteem, Coping with Life, Eating Disorders, Money and Stress.

CHAPTER ONE:

FEELINGS
Looking and feeling different

Your teenage years should be the best in your life, but often they are plagued by inner turmoil, insecurity and difficult relationships. So much is expected of you, yet you seem less capable of handling anything.

Some of this inability to cope with the changes within, physical changes and changing expectations, is down to what's happening to your body and brain. In the first years of puberty, rapid rises in the level of sex hormones affect body growth and maturity, and the way you think and act.

Girls often get moody, irritable and a bit down, all reactions to hormones. Fluctuations in oestrogen and progesterone during the menstrual cycle can lead to PMS (pre-menstrual syndrome). Increases in testosterone can make boys become aggressive and rash – and think about sex a lot of the time!

As well as changes created by sex hormones, there's the added complication of your reaction to them. Many teenagers feel self-conscious about what's happening to their bodies. Not everyone's comfortable with breasts and erections. Experiencing these changes – often all at once – can make girls and boys think they're abnormal. But puberty occurs at different ages and varying speeds. Everyone develops and reacts in different ways.

The way you develop depends on hormonal activity, nutrition, gender and inherent characteristics. In the same way you may have inherited your mother's or father's eye colour, you are also likely to start your period when your mother did or have an adult penis a similar size to your father's.

FACT BOX

The trigger for puberty in both boys and girls is the production of gonadotrophin releasing hormone (GnRH). This hormone stimulates the pituitary gland to release two hormones, follicle stimulating hormone (FSH) and luteinizing hormone (LH). These 'switch on' sexual maturity. As puberty progresses, a girl's ovaries begin releasing oestrogen and progesterone and a boy's testicles start secreting testosterone.

Puberty for boys

■ Puberty starts when the body makes testosterone. This happens between the ages of 11 and 16, although changes can continue to 19.

- Boys' voices break (get deeper). The voice box grows larger and changes shape. This usually takes months, but it can happen overnight.

- Body shape changes as bones and muscles thicken.

- Genitals change. Testicles (balls) grow bigger and the penis gets longer and wider. Testicles aren't the same size and it's normal to feel a lumpy part on one side – the epididymis.

- Boys have erections. Blood rushes into the penis and it hardens and lengthens. Erections point towards the belly button away from the body. Some bend upwards or to one side. Boys can learn to control erections by thinking of something non-sexual.

- Boys ejaculate (orgasm, climax, come/cum). This starts between 10 and 18, most often at 13 or 14. Boys may first ejaculate when asleep (wet dreams) or during masturbation (wanking). Ejaculation is when semen (containing sperm) spurts or dribbles out of the hole at the top of the penis. Boys ejaculate when sexually excited, and this feels good – an orgasm.

- Hair grows in different places – armpits, face and genitals.

- Spots appear and sweat is produced. Everyone should wash genitals and underarms every day. It's good to keep skin clean but over-washing with harsh products (used to control spots) can actually increase the production of sebum (grease). Harsh products containing soap, detergent or perfume can also cause sensitive reactions in the genital area.

FACT BOX

When boys' testosterone levels reach a certain level, the excess is converted into the female hormone, oestrogen. Oestrogen is necessary for the health and growth of bones.

Puberty for Girls

- Puberty starts when the body makes oestrogen and progesterone. This happens between the ages of 8 and 14, although changes can continue up to 18.

- At puberty a girl's body shape becomes curvier, as oestrogen triggers the laying down of fat. Usually by 14 the spine has finished growing and pelvic bones widen and smoothen, ready for childbirth.

- Breasts appear. Once the ovaries send oestrogen around the body, a girl's breasts begin to grow. This is gradual, sometimes taking four years. The first sign is when nipples stand out.

- Female sex organs grow. Those on the inside are called reproductive organs, and those outside are genitals. The vulva (opening to the vagina, the clitoris and lips surrounding the clitoris) develops.

- Periods start. Monthly bleeding from the vagina first begins during puberty and continues until a woman is in her forties or fifties. It can take time for regular egg production and periods to settle down. The start of bleeding doesn't signal the ability to conceive, as an egg isn't always released for the first month. Some girls release eggs for several months before bleeding.

- Hair grows in different places – armpits, face, legs and genitals.

- Spots appear and sweat is produced. Everyone should wash genitals and underarms every day. It's good to keep skin clean but over-washing with harsh products (used to control spots) can actually increase the production of sebum (grease). Harsh products containing soap, detergent or perfume can also cause sensitive reactions in the genital area.

How you think about yourself is the biggest change of all. This can fluctuate from feeling you're the greatest, most gorgeous creature that walked the earth, to feeling like pond life.

Changes in the way you feel, react and look are indications of sex hormone activity in the same way that pubic hair, erections and periods are. If the great ups and downs of puberty get you down, you can take positive action to even out the effect of hormonal imbalances.

Handling hormones

- Don't miss meals – especially breakfast – it can make you tired and grumpy. Eat something nutritious every four hours, but avoid sweets and fatty foods.

- Sleep is essential. While you sleep a growth hormone is released. You actually need more sleep than children and adults and missing out will make you tired and emotional. Explain to Mum and Dad those weekend lie-ins are necessary!

- Exercise will make you feel better. Hormones released when exercising can improve fluctuating moods. Try half-an-hour's exercise at least three times a week – a brisk walk, a kick around with a ball or cycling to school is great. You don't have to join a gym.

- Alcohol is a depressant. It can make you feel down and aggressive. It also dehydrates, leading to tiredness, lack of concentration and irritability. The lower your body weight, the quicker you'll get drunk.

- Drinks like cola, tea and coffee contain caffeine, which gives your body an unnatural high, followed by a low. Choose decaf tea and coffee and cut down on cola.

- Nicotine is an appetite suppressant, so smoking can lead to missed meals. Cigarette smoking can lead to a dependency on the effects of nicotine and long-term physical damage.

- Smoking cannabis (dope) can make you feel listless, depressed and paranoid as well as affecting your concentration.

- Girls can try evening primrose oil or starflower oil if you feel worse before or during a period, and ask your doctor about B6 tablets. If you have heavy periods and feel tired all the time you may lack iron. Get advice from your GP.

MANAGING THE MAYHEM

Increased hormones are not the only reason why you may feel confident in the morning but crushed by the afternoon. As you mature you'll feel increasingly more like an adult and will expect to be treated like one. This can result in conflict with family, friends and authority figures.

FACT BOX

Scientists studying changes in the adolescent brain discovered the emotional region of the brain develops to maturity ahead of the part controlling rational thought. Teenagers have well-developed emotions and feelings, but often don't have the ability or experience to think things through properly.

Teenagers are often portrayed as rebellious, fun-seeking, reckless creatures with an overwhelming interest in sex and a disregard for authority and routine. In fact, teenagers express a natural curiosity about the adult world, and the need to assert an emerging character and independence on it.

Feeling down

Not all teenagers experience growing up in the same way. Some sail through adolescence serenely, while others drag themselves through kicking and screaming. Most teenagers handle moodiness and moroseness, which subside with increasing age and self-confidence.

However, some young people become depressed and stay depressed. The causes of (diagnosed) teenage depression can include: stress at school or work; difficult family life; lack of confidence and low self-esteem; or an inherent tendency to depression.

FACT BOX

Suicide accounts for 20 per cent of all deaths among young people aged 15–24 and is the second most common cause of death among young people. Seventy-five per cent of suicides in the UK are by men and there are now 67 per cent more suicides in men aged 15–24 than there were in 1982. Young women aged 15–19 are at the highest risk of attempted suicide.

Source: www.mind.org.uk

If you feel worried that your state of mind is spiralling downward, ask for help: you will be taken seriously. Helpful Organisations gives details on where to go for support and advice, or just someone to talk to.

Feeling dangerous

Most teenagers indulge in some dangerous, unhealthy or anti-social pursuits. But, although we hear an increasing amount about anti-social activity, drug and drink misuse and driving offences, most people get through their teenage years without breaking the law.

FACT BOX

Young men are more likely to be arrested than anyone else in society. However, statistics show that for most boys, criminal behaviour begins around the age of 13, peaks at 17 and disappears in early adulthood.

Source: www.bbc.co.uk/science

Their behaviour can alienate teenagers from the people around them, leading to conflict and difficulties in relationships. It won't only be parents or teachers who react to the new and different ways you behave, it may be friends too. As you assert yourself, adults may think you're growing up too quickly and friends may be confused by your actions.

The secret is to be yourself and be confident. Sometimes that means having the confidence to say, 'No, that doesn't feel right, that's not what I want.' Sometimes it means saying: 'I was wrong, I'm sorry.'

'Sometimes I used to think, "why the hell did I say or do that?" It's like being out of control. Then one day you wake up and you're in control. You know how you feel and you feel OK. It's just getting there that's the drag!' **Gee, 18**

It's difficult to know what you do feel and what you do want when your mood swings from calm and collected to seeing the world through a red mist. Here are some tips to help you get by.

■ Avoid impulsive acts and answers. If you think you may explode – into anger or tears – walk away, count to ten or do something else.

■ Listen to your instincts. If you feel something isn't right, follow your gut feeling.

■ Communicate. People aren't mind readers: you need to tell them how you feel. It's not silly or wimpish to talk about emotions; it's the brave and intelligent thing to do.

■ Don't be taken in by bravado – other people feel insecure too.

■ Don't brood alone. Feeling down or moody is normal, but if you're desperate, depressed, suicidal or inclined to self harm, get help (see Helpful Organisations).

Feeling sexy

As sex hormones kick in you'll start to think of yourself as a sexual being. Feeling sexy or thinking about sex will become part of life. It's natural for everyone to become more sexually aware, but it doesn't mean you are ready to have sex.

FANTASIES

Teenagers spend a lot of time thinking and talking about sex, but most spend far more time imagining sexual encounters than experiencing them.

Fantasising (daydreaming) about sex is one way of exploring future real-life situations or imagining ones you'd never be involved with in real life. The advantage of fantasy is that it's not reality, so let your imagination run riot.

SEXUALITY

Sexual orientation (or sexuality) means your sexual feelings towards males and females. It's common to have feelings towards or fantasies about people of the same sex. If you imagine kissing a friend, teacher or stranger of the same sex it doesn't mean you're gay or bisexual, it can be part of emerging sexual awareness. However, if your feelings towards people of the same sex deepen over time and you begin to question your sexuality, you may want to explore it further. See Chapter 4 for more information.

MASTURBATION

Exploring your urges on your own is part of growing up and learning about your sexual responses. Masturbation is sexual pleasure you give to yourself. No one can tell if you masturbate and everyone does it – male or female, gay or straight. No harm will come to you or anyone else if you pleasure yourself, as long as you do it in private and no-one is exploited.

Some religions and cultures forbid masturbation. They believe that sex is for procreation (making babies) only, and not for recreation, which includes pleasuring yourself. However, masturbation is not bad for your physical or mental health: in fact, it may have positive benefits, including relieving stress.

Masturbation techniques

- A boy usually masturbates by wrapping his hand around the shaft of his penis, moving his fingers and thumb up and down the head (top part) until he ejaculates (comes). The head of the penis is the most sensitive area, but it's also pleasurable for boys' nipples and scrotum (ball sac) to be touched. There are different ways to masturbate, so it's normal to experiment.

■ A girl usually masturbates by stimulating her clitoris, either directly or indirectly. The clitoris is part of a girl's external genitals at the top of the opening to the vagina. A girl gets a lovely feeling when the clitoris is gently rubbed and this can lead to orgasm (coming). There are different ways to masturbate and girls may like to touch breasts or put a finger inside the vagina. Find out what feels good for you.

CHAPTER TWO:

FAMILIES
How to cope at home

> '*It's always been just me and Mum. As I grew up she realised she was losing me and panicked. She treated me like a child because she didn't want to let go. I understood her but it didn't always make it easier to deal with.*' **James, 15**

One of the biggest deals throughout teenage years is home life. Even for those with a supportive, settled and peaceful family, once hormones and adult expectations appear, life at home can become hell – for everyone.

Those closest to you will experience the new you at first hand and will have the hardest job adapting to this changing child. Look at it from their point of view: They thought they knew the son/daughter/ brother/sister living in the house, but a creature appears who:

- spends most of the day asleep
- spends hours in the bedroom or bathroom
- plays loud music all day and most of the night
- doesn't talk, just grunts and shouts
- won't go on family outings, or stay in the same room watching TV
- doesn't eat properly, just starves or binges
- dresses funny and smells funny
- hangs out with gangs until all hours doing – well – nothing!

TIME TO TALK

Parents usually act out of love. They know how tricky and dangerous the adult world can be, and seeing you entering it is scary. It's difficult to think about things from their point of view when so much is going on in your head, but give them a chance to understand how you think and feel.

You'll want to spend more time hanging out with mates and in your own room, which means less opportunity to interact with the family. Having time and space to yourself becomes more important, but families might think you're shunning them or sulking. They may be concerned that something is wrong.

The only way to get them off your back is to tell them how you feel, what you need and what you would like them to do. The best way to do this is calmly, clearly and logically. A sign on your bedroom door saying 'KEEP OUT' won't help!

You may not want cosy chats with your parents about emotions, but communicating effectively with them will help everyone get through this time of transition.

Top communication tips

■ Don't talk when you're angry. Wait until you feel cool, calm and collected.

■ Pick the right moment – when everyone has time, there are no distractions and the mood is calm. If making an appointment sounds heavy, get your mum/dad on her/his own by offering to go shopping with them or helping prepare a meal.

■ Know how you feel. Ask yourself why you react in a certain way. It's fine to say, 'It just doesn't feel right', or 'It makes me feel uncomfortable'.

■ Don't worry about knowing your lines – you don't need to plan a speech or be precise about what you're going to say; just get across the important points. If you need to collect your thoughts, ask them to give you a minute.

■ Listen to what they have to say – they might say something useful! Good communicating is about listening. You don't have to agree with everything, but give them a chance to speak.

■ Let them help – it's hard for parents to hear you're upset or frustrated. Think about something they can do for you, even if it's just giving you space at home on certain days.

■ Be honest. Tell them how you feel and give them a chance to try to understand.

■ Make it positive – finish the chat with a promise, plan or action that will make a difference. Try to agree a new way of looking at things or a new way of doing something.

Parents aren't mind readers, so let them know how you feel before it becomes a big issue. Connecting well with parents – and communicating in a mature way – can lead to real understanding and respect in teenage family relationships. Shutting out those closest to you leads to misunderstanding and hostility, and can spiral into relationship breakdowns.

BRAVING THE BATTLEFIELD

Sometimes things go too far. And when it's war at home and every day brings a new battle, connecting with parents is difficult.

Tips for managing angry encounters

- If you know you get angry and emotional, count to ten as soon as you feel your blood pressure rising. Take deep breaths. Think about what you're going to say and how best to say it.

- It's fine to say 'me' in conversations, but keep 'you' out of a discussion. Blaming and getting personal won't help. Keep the words 'always' and 'never' out of the conversation. Don't attack and don't be defensive.

- When asking parents for something or negotiating with them, make sure you have an argument that will stand up. Think about it in advance and practise it before you say it.

- Make sure the argument stands up on its own merits. Saying, 'So-and-so's mum lets her/him do it, so I don't see why I can't', didn't work when you were ten and it won't work now.

- If you know it's an issue, tell them. Try saying, 'I know we've argued about this in the past, but I'd like to...'

- Be prepared for questions. Parents may want proof you've thought about it. If you can't answer, don't get angry, just say, 'I'm not sure about that, I'll think about it/find out about it and get back to you.'

- Most negotiations involve bargaining. Be willing to compromise and settle for something everyone's happy with. For instance, 'I know I wanted to stay at the party until 1am, but as you're not happy with that, perhaps I could stay until midnight if you come and pick me up?'

- Say you've thought of their point of view – you may think it's unreasonable, but try to understand why they think like that. Don't tell them they're being mean/stupid. If you don't respect their point of view, why should they respect yours?

■ Listening is important. Have your say, but let them have theirs too. Don't shout them down.

■ Talk quietly and slowly – even if their voice is raised. This will calm things down and make you sound mature and sensible.

■ If you can't go a whole conversation without confrontation and end up saying things you regret, apologise.

Anger can flare up in a moment, or it can be a constant state of mind. When hormones fluctuate emotions are near the surface. Sometimes anger is the least embarrassing emotion to display – shouting is better than bawling. But it can get you into trouble and it can mean issues go unresolved. If you need to keep anger in check and aggression out of relationships, give yourself time and space to manage it.

'Mum and I used to argue every day. I didn't even know what we were saying. I had to make her see how things were different. She just didn't understand how much I'd changed.' **Ben, 16**

Managing emotions

■ Try deep breathing, meditation, yoga or Pilates to handle long-term stress and aggression.

■ Relax your body as your emotions start stirring. Concentrate on each muscle from your toes up or your ears down. Unclench teeth and fists and uncross arms and legs.

- Slow down your breathing and breathe from your chest and stomach.

- Listen to chill-out music and relax, or get into some happy sounds and dance around your bedroom. Singing opens up the throat and deepens breathing, so switch on the karaoke. Steer clear of loud, violent music with thumping beats.

- Don't beat up pillows, scream, shout, or hit out to exorcise aggression – it creates more adrenaline.

- Get some exercise. The hormones released with vigorous exercise promote calm. Try swimming, cycling, running, dancing, athletics or team sports.

- Be nice to yourself. Look in the mirror and tell yourself what a great person you are.

Parents may seem like the enemy but they want to understand what you're going through and help you through it. Everyone needs love, understanding and support in times of stress. You may feel you're adult enough to go it alone, but they still have a role as your safety net – and they are legally responsible for you until you're 18.

If you have serious family problems, turn to Helpful Organisations for groups that can help.

CHAPTER THREE:

FRIENDS
Friendships are important

Being a teenager can be trying when relationships change and people are distant. But these years are when genuine, lasting relationships are built. In moving away from the close bond of the family, you move towards people of your own age who can identify with how you feel. The emphasis in your life shifts from home to outside the family, with mates at the centre of your universe.

When you're aged 12–20 your peers exert the most influence on your life. Even if you have a great family, friends will still be the ones who teach you most about the world – and yourself. People learn about life through relationships and those experiences shape our views, behaviour and who we are.

MOVING ON

When you're a young teenager, established friendships can be put to the test. The gap between childhood and adulthood widens and friends of the opposite sex and a different age may change their attitude towards you. Even your best friends may not seem as straightforward or reliable as they did before. Your friends from primary school may not be as close as you grow up.

> *'I've had a best friend all my life and she's a year older. Now we're not so close any more. Sometimes the way she talks to me is annoying. It's as if she thinks she's much older. It upsets me that it's changed.'* **Mel, 12**

You will be changing – in looks, opinions and tastes – and sometimes those changes are just not compatible with certain friendships. Making new friends and saying goodbye to old ones is a natural part of moving on, so try not to be too sad about it.

Boys and girls

For girls, friends are people:

- you share secrets, fears and insecurities with
- you gossip with about boys and your love life
- you discuss fashion and music with
- you always have a lot to chat about with
- you stand by at all costs!

For boys, friends are people:

- you play or watch football with
- you play and listen to music with
- you hang out and have a laugh with
- you call when you're bored.

'When we're all boys in a crowd we're dudes, we have a laugh. Girls take everything more seriously – they get sensitive. Boys just aren't like that. We mess about.'   **Ali, 14**

For girls, the security of a close friendship is constructive as long as it's working well, but because girls invest so much honesty and emotion in friendships, when they go wrong it can be heart-breaking. Sharing everything with your best mate is great, but if you fall out, the whole school gets to know.

Resolving issues within friendships is also different. Boys will have an argument (and sometimes a punch-up), then move on, but girls often wage psychological warfare, sulking and holding grudges for a very long time.

Friends provide companionship and support and form social groups that share values and beliefs. Good friendships can make all the difference to how you make it through teenage traumas.

How to have smart friendships

■ Listen to your instinct when you meet people for the first time. Don't stop at first impressions, but remember how you felt and what you thought about your 'new friend'.

■ Don't be seduced by appearances. The coolest, loudest and most popular girl/boy in the school won't necessarily be the most trustworthy and genuine friend.

■ Don't put all your eggs in one basket – investing all your time, energy and emotion in just one person makes heartache more likely.

■ Don't feel you can only be real friends with people of the same sex. Having an opposite-sex friend can be great fun – and an insight!

■ Don't worry if you don't have close friendships or many friends. You may not always have the opportunity to meet your sort of people. You don't have to force friendships.

■ Real friends don't make you do things you don't want to, they care about what you think and how you feel. They are willing to listen and to compromise. And so should you be!

HOW GOOD A FRIEND ARE YOU?

Being a good friend is hard work. It means being unselfish and understanding – the basis of a good friendship is treating your friend as you would like to be treated yourself.

To find out if you're a good friend, do the quiz below. Solutions are at the end of this chapter.

ARE YOU A GOOD FRIEND?

1 You're in a shoe shop and notice that a pair your friend has been saving up for is in the sale. There's only one pair left and it's in your size – the same as your friend's. Do you:

a Call her/him on the mobile and tell her/him to get over here now!

b Put the shoes to one side, then go to your friend's house and fetch her/him.

c Try to remember to mention the sale next time you see her/him.

2 You and your friend have been set a joint school project. On the afternoon when you've arranged to do the work, your friend rings up and says she/he's got a date and can't make it. She/he asks you to do the work and make out you did it together. Do you:

a Swear down the phone and tell her/him you're no longer friends.

b Tell her/him you'll do it just this once but never again.

c Try to persuade your friend to postpone the date so you can do the work together.

3 You're in the skate park and you hear some girls bitching about your best friend. Do you:

a Skate near them so you can eavesdrop and report back to your friend.

b Join them and stick up for her/him.

c Walk away and say nothing to anyone.

4 Your friend has gone out with someone on a motorbike for the evening. They know their parents don't approve, so asked you to cover. Late that night you get a phone call from his/her mum/dad asking if your friend is with you. Do you:

a Say yes, he/she's in the loo and will call back later, then try to track him/her down.

b Say he/she's out but you don't know where.

c Tell the parent as much as you know because it's late and you're worried, then face your friend later.

5 A new boyfriend/girlfriend asks you out on a night when it's your best friend's birthday celebration. Do you:

a Tell her/him you're busy but can make it another night.

b Tell her/him you're celebrating with a friend and you'll ask if she/he can join you.

c Tell her/him, 'it's a date!'

6 A boy/girl you know your friend is mad about has made a move on you. Do you:

a Ring up your friend and say 'guess what just happened...'

b Say you'll go out with him/her – because you really like them too.

c Say 'no, thanks, but do you know ... fancies you?'

Learning to appreciate the value of sound friendships is part of growing up. Spotting when friends are not worth the investment and when peer pressure is squashing your personality is an important lesson too.

PEER PRESSURE

FACT BOX

Teenagers aged 11–14 seem more influenced by peer pressure than older teenagers.

Peer pressure means being made to conform to the 'norm' of the group you are in, whether the people involved are friends, classmates or other members of a club.

Peer pressure doesn't have to be heavy. Sometimes you just know that unless you do something, you'll be left out. Everyone wants to be accepted, but you also want to be appreciated for who you are and what you think.

Most of the time peer pressure is a harmless part of growing up and making friends. However, if peer pressure makes you do things against your will or behave in a way you know is wrong, it's time to make a stand.

Often peers become influential because you've lost contact with your family or you've broken up with friends. It's easy to be swayed by others when you're feeling hurt or alone. If you are having trouble, get support from someone close you can talk to – family or friends. Sometimes you just need another person to look objectively at what's happening, sometimes you need someone to back you up.

BULLYING

Bullying can make life a misery. It can make you miss school or do badly when you are there, lose confidence and self-esteem and even make you physically ill. Bullying should not be tolerated.

FACT BOX

Around 16 children in the UK kill themselves every year after being bullied. **Source: www.bullyonline.org**

What is bullying?

There are three kinds of bullying:

■ **physical bullying** includes hitting, punching, slapping, hair pulling and pushing

■ **verbal bullying** includes name-calling, racist and sexist comments, swearing and unkind jokes

■ **relational bullying** means being left out or having nasty gossip spread about you.

Bullying is defined by its effect on the person being bullied: one teenager may see some behaviour as playful fun, while another will find it frightening. Many teenagers experience teasing and name-calling and most can handle it. But if you're feeling low or insecure, it can be hurtful.

Beating bullies

■ **Act confidently** – hold up your head, stride out, don't slouch and shuffle.

■ **Hang around with friends** – bullies usually approach lone people, not groups.

■ **Tackle the problem** – if you're being bullied and suspect others are too, build a case against the bully together, and report it.

Handling bullies on your own is difficult, but if you're being harmed (physically or emotionally) you need to tell them. If that doesn't stop them, you need to tell someone else.

All schools have a bullying policy and adults are much more aware of bullying issues now, so report your problem. If you're being seriously victimised or physically hurt, go straight to the police. Never feel ashamed to report a bully. Bullying is never the fault of the person who is being bullied.

If you'd like more information on bullying, see Helpful Organisations for a list of groups and websites that can help.

> **For a closer look at bullying see**
> ***Real Life Issues – Bullying.***

Quiz answers

1 **a** That's the nicest thing to do. Even if she/he can't get to the shop, you've given her/him the opportunity to get the shoes, and you've shown you're thinking of her/him.

b A sensible solution – and you're putting yourself out for your friend, which will be appreciated.

c You're not really thinking of your friend, are you? All friendships need a bit of effort and kindness.

2 **a** What an angry reaction! Not only will you lose a friend, but the homework won't get done either. Look for a solution and talk it through.

b You're being loyal to a friend by helping them out – but are you really helping? She/he will miss schoolwork, which may lead to difficulty in class. Also, you have given an ultimatum that next time you'll have to honour – which means losing a friend or being a doormat.

c A calm, civilised and rational conversation may convince your friend she/he is not doing the right thing. You'll need a back-up plan, however, in case it doesn't!

3 **a** You may want to know what they're saying so you or your friend can refute it, but is it in their best interests to know what's been said? Think about how your friend might react. Will they be hurt, angry, mortified? Sometimes it's best to leave things alone.

b It's all very well getting stuck in like a loyal friend, but isn't that going to inflame the situation? If you react and confront the girls, you'll have to tell your friend what they said. Also, something that might have been quickly forgotten will get all around the school.

c Discretion may be the better part of valour. Unkind words have no strength if they are ignored.

4 **a** Lying is not going to help anyone – especially if you can't contact your friend.

b That's not being a good friend. Not only are you dropping your friend in it, but you're not helping her/his parents either.

c It's in everyone's best interests for you to tell the truth. You'd never forgive yourself if something happened to your friend. If they can't see that what you did was right and caring, they're not such a great mate.

5 **a** You're busy and you can make it another night, so what's the big deal? If she/he can't accept that your friend's birthday comes first, she/he is not worth going out with!

b A good solution. Being honest with your date and considerate with your friend is the best way to behave.

c What kind of a friend are you?

6

a You're not a nice friend!

b If you really like the person, then it's fair to want to accept – you're doing no wrong. However, it might save on hurt and upset later if you talk it through with your friend.

c That's a kind, if not casual way to deal with the situation. If the date really likes you, she/he may be offended or embarrassed. If your friend really likes your date she/he may be offended or embarrassed! If you do want to decline, just do it kindly and politely – and keep your mouth shut!

CHAPTER FOUR:

JUST GOOD FRIENDS?
Fancying and flirting

You may have fancied boys or girls as a junior, but dating really starts from Year 7 when the difference between being attracted to someone and liking her/him as a friend becomes clear.

When you fancy someone:
- your heart beats faster when you see them
- you get all tongue-tied and nervous when you're with them.
- you have sexual fantasies about them
- you want to kiss them
- you want to see them whenever you can.

Often the objects of desire are unattainable. They might be too old, too popular (sometimes everyone fancies the same girl/boy at school), attached, or just unavailable – like Orlando Bloom or Keira Knightley. An attraction to an unattainable person can be the extension of a fantasy life.

The most genuine attractions and relationships are those within your own peer group. Often teenagers start to feel differently about friends, and a relationship based on a long-standing friendship can work well. However, once you've been dating someone it's difficult to go back to being 'just good friends'. Attraction can be fleeting and sometimes friendships are so solid and valuable, they're just not worth risking.

First date tips

■ If you don't know your date well, meet for lunch or after school. If the date is a disaster, you can escape with an excuse to be somewhere else.

■ Be safe. Meet in daylight and let your parents (or someone responsible) know where you're going and when you'll be back. Take your mobile.

■ If you're nervous or unsure, take a friend along. You can introduce them and ask your friend to stay for a short while or get your friend to watch you from a distance. Arrange a (subtle) signal between you beforehand, so you can tell her/him when it's OK to leave.

■ If you're worried about conversation, pick a venue where talk is limited. Go to an event like a football match or a gig. The theatre and cinema are great too, but meet up before the show – otherwise you'll never get to know one another!

Some people – usually older – offer teenagers the promise of a fantasy life come true and a grown-up relationship. Teenagers – especially younger ones – should be aware of the dangers in this. 'Grooming' (befriending and winning the trust of) young people can lead to sexual exploitation and abuse.

Be wary of older people who try to attract you – socially, via friends and family and the Internet. Never meet anyone you don't know well (especially a 'friend' from a chatroom) on your own or without informing an adult. For further information and advice turn to Helpful Organisations.

ATTRACTING ATTENTION

Sometimes it's difficult attracting the right sort of attention from the right person. Flirting in a subtle and appropriate way sends out the right signals without embarrassment or rejection. If that special person flirts back, you're in with a chance!

How to be a fab flirt

- Believe you can do it! You don't have to be an extrovert to flirt. Internally you can be a mess and outwardly exude confidence and sex appeal.

- Look confident! Stand tall, head up and shoulders back, facing the person you are flirting with.

- Look friendly! To be approached look approachable. Wear unthreatening clothes – nothing too sexy or scary fashion statements! Uncross your arms and legs, and *smile*.

- Make eye contact! Catching someone's eye for a few seconds is all you need to do. If it's hard to make direct eye contact, look at different features of their face, take in their ears, neck, hair, eyebrows, mouth and nose.

- Be enthralled! You don't have to hold their gaze all the time – but keep coming back to their eyes. If they're talking about something important to them, hold their gaze – there's nothing more attractive than feeling someone only has eyes for you.

- Be a mirror image! Adopt the same positions and gestures as your flirting partner – it helps you connect.

- Breathe! Take deep breaths to calm down and slow your heart. Breathing deeply before speaking lowers your voice, making you sound mature and in control.

- Speak slowly and clearly – and not all the time! The more calm and in control you sound, the more at ease and confident your flirting partner will be. Don't fill all the gaps in conversation.

- Be inclusive! Include his/her name in your conversation and continue conversations by saying, 'as I was telling you ...'

- Accept compliments! Say 'thank you' graciously, smile, and continue the conversation. Don't disagree with the compliment and don't feel vain for accepting it. And just because you've had a compliment, you don't have to give one back.

Flirting doesn't have to lead anywhere. Sparking up a flirtatious connection can be fun and flattering – for both of you. Don't ever feel that just because you've had a good flirt you're obliged to take it further.

GIRLS ARE FROM VENUS, BOYS ARE FROM MARS

The way boys and girls view dating and relationships can be agonisingly different. Here are some examples of what the sexes think of dating.

Boys on going out with girls:
'It annoys me girls don't make the first move. They expect you to do everything. I'd love it if a girl came up to me and said: "I really like you, want to go out sometime?" Why do boys have to be rejected?'

'Girls get all kissy and cuddly, then get annoyed when you take it further. They just want to have a boy to show off to their friends, they're not interested in it for real.'

'I can't bear girls who hang around all the time, expect you to call or text all the time and won't let you go out with your mates. Girls can be soppy and jealous, and it's a turn-off.'

Girls on going out with boys:
'Boys have double standards. They say they like flirty, forward girls,
but if you make a move on them you're a slag!'

'Boys think it's OK to have sex with anyone they want to, but if a girl
has done it with someone – just one boy – she gets a bad
reputation.'

'I went out with a boy for four months, then he just disappeared. I
had to hear it from his mates that he didn't want to see me anymore.
It made me feel stupid and I was left wondering what I did wrong.'

Men and women often want different things from relationships and it
can take time to figure out whether either of you will be satisfied with
what's on offer.

Dating can go wrong because:
- you like her/him but your friends don't approve. Your friends may
  not like you spending time with your girlfriend/boyfriend instead of
  them
- you like her/him but your parents don't approve. Your parents may
  think you should be studying. They may not think the girlfriend/
  boyfriend is good enough for you
- you like her/him more than she/he likes you – or vice versa
- you may want a long-term relationship with commitment and
  monogamy – she/he may want some fun with no future.

The way to get over these obstacles is to communicate – say what
you think, but be sensitive to your partner's feelings. Look at the tips
on communication and negotiation in Chapter 1.

Boys and girls do think and feel differently about relationships. Be tolerant of different expectations, but never tolerate behaviour that forces you to do something you don't want to. You shouldn't be afraid to speak up honestly about how you feel.

SAME-SEX ATTRACTION

Just because you like or fancy someone of the same sex, it doesn't mean you're gay. Many teenagers who have crushes on people of the same sex never have same-sex relationships.

What is sexuality?

■ Your sexuality is who you are as a sexual being. Sexuality usually refers to whether someone is straight (heterosexual) or gay (homosexual). Homosexuals are attracted to people of the same sex, while bisexuals are attracted to both sexes. Homosexual women are often called lesbians and men are called gays, although 'gay' is also a general term.

■ Telling people about your sexuality is called 'coming out'. It's a good idea to find out people's attitudes on sexuality before talking to them.

■ Homophobia (fear of or prejudice against gay people) is sadly common. Many young gay people find it difficult getting friends and family to understand.

■ You don't have to tell anyone you're gay if you don't want to, but if you want to live openly as a gay person, you have to come out. Many gay people start by telling a close friend or relation, then gradually tell more people. Many gay teenagers find it most difficult to tell their parents.

■ Being gay doesn't mean you will never have steady relationships or a family. Many gay couples have relationships that last decades. Gay men and women are able to adopt children and in some countries gay couples can marry.

> Being gay doesn't make it more likely someone will get AIDS.
> Everyone who has sex needs to be aware of sexually transmitted
> infections (STIs): see Chapter 7.

Sexual identities develop over time and it may take years to
understand your sexuality. Boys and girls with real gay feelings find
their attraction to people of the same sex becomes clearer. People
often recognise their homosexuality during puberty and teen-hood.

FACT BOX

*About one in ten people in the
world is homosexual – the same
proportion that's naturally blonde.*

How do I know I'm gay?

If you think you might be gay, ask yourself:

- when I dream or fantasize sexually, is it about boys or girls?
- have I ever had a crush or been in love with someone of the same
  sex?
- do I feel different from the girls and boys I hang out with?
- do I feel uncomfortable when it starts getting sexual with the
  opposite sex?

Trust your instincts and don't be ashamed of who you are. Gay people
are all around, and you will meet someone who feels the same way
you do.

Getting in touch with gay helplines or organisations can be useful: you'll find out more about gay life and make contact with other gay teenagers. See Helpful Organisations for contacts.

'It's only recently I've admitted I'm gay. I've known for over ten years, but have never come to terms with it. I've had relationships with women but they've never been right. I live in a small village and I just couldn't bear the thought of people's attitudes. But I'm much happier now I can be who I really am.' **Steve, 27**

Becoming a healthy sexual gay man or woman is part of coming out. Sex should happen between mature individuals who care about each other and understand the responsibilities. If you don't feel ready, explore your sexual needs by masturbating and fantasising.

People choose to have sex in different ways, whether gay or straight. Gay men and women can give pleasure by mutual masturbation, oral sex, anal intercourse, kissing, hugging, massage, cuddling or anything else that both people are happy with.

Being gay in a world that doesn't always understand or accept homosexuality is not easy. If you know you're gay, you may choose not to tell people until you're older. However, coming out may make you feel much better about yourself. Most teenagers who accept their sexuality say they are calmer, happier and more confident. Self-denial and living a lie can be personally damaging as well as difficult day-to-day. Even if you keep your sexuality a secret from other people, you need to be honest with yourself.

CHAPTER FIVE:

ROMANTIC RELATIONSHIPS
That special person

Before settling down with someone, you need to discover who you are as a partner, lover and adult. Romantic relationships have a much better chance of success and survival if you have a strong sense of self. Knowing who you are – your strengths and weaknesses, your values, likes and dislikes and the type of emotional environment that allows you to grow – makes solid foundations for a relationship.

FACT BOX

Men who are in love have lower levels of the male sex hormone testosterone – linked to aggression and sex drive – than other men. Love-struck women, in contrast, had higher levels of testosterone than their counterparts.

Source: ***New Scientist*** **2004**

Once you've established who you are, it's time to find out how your partner matches your personality, expectations and principles. Don't go into a relationship thinking you can change a person: it just doesn't happen. Knowing what you're prepared to accept means you can compromise without losing integrity.

Relationships require constant negotiation and re-negotiation and it's important to know your bottom line. Girls and boys who get walked over in relationships are usually unsure of what they want or what they're prepared to accept. There are no hard and fast rules in love. You just have to live your values – what's OK for you may be out of order for a friend, and vice versa.

'I don't need a relationship to make me happy. I most definitely don't hate men at all. But I have a radar for bad guys. It might be one thing he says, but I'm quick to take notice.'
Missy Elliott (Quote courtesy of *Glamour* magazine and Warner Bros Music, 2004)

It's not easy to understand what another person feels or why they feel it, but you do need to accept it. If someone tells you honestly how she/he feels, then it's valid. Respecting one another's feelings and reactions is a measure of your love – and a way of getting to know someone well.

'I used to treat girls badly – tell 'em you love 'em, then leave 'em. But when I was 16 I fell in love, really in love. It was bliss for a while, then she left me. God, was I hurt! I would never want to hurt anyone else like that now.' **Gee, 18**

Being able to talk to your partner is the strongest indication that you have a chance as a couple. If you communicate honestly and respectfully, you will always be able to solve problems together.

MOVING ON

Each relationship is different and every relationship shifts as it evolves. That's particularly true if you're a teenager. As you find out more about yourself, your relationship will either change or be out of synch with who you are. It's normal to grow out of teenage loves, so don't be afraid to move on.

Moving on may mean breaking up and that's difficult. If there's good, open communication between you, telling someone it's over will be an extension of your relationship. If communication is difficult, you need to think about the best way to make your feelings known.

How to tell her/him how you feel:

■ Face-to-face honesty is good, but not always appropriate. You have to feel comfortable talking about the small stuff first.

- A heavy conversation won't work if you're not that close. Try a short note and make it simple.

- Don't pour your heart out in a letter if it might be passed around.

- Make sure she/he gets the news before anyone else.

- Say something positive: don't make it all negative.

- In face-to-face break-ups pick the right time and place.

- Think about the consequences. What will happen afterwards? Be sensible.

- If you have doubts about your plan, check it out with a friend.

- Honesty is usually the best policy, but always be sensitive.

FALLING IN LOVE

'When it's lust you just want to have sex with someone, but love is different. I'm only in love with one girl. You know when it's love, I can't explain, you just know.'

Spike, 15

Love is amazing. Love is the ultimate happy fix we all want to experience. There is nothing so fantastic as that feeling when you really adore someone and they love you madly back. Nothing beats knowing you're the most important person in someone's life.

What is love?

- a chemical reaction

- a mad passion

- an overwhelming tenderness

- being loveable

- ultimate trust and respect

- finding a soul-mate

- putting someone else first

- making someone happy

- sharing yourself

- wanting to be together, forever.

It doesn't matter how others define love, we each love in different ways. Love is flexible, it can expand and contract to fit any two people in any situation at any time.

'I thought love was explosive, but it isn't always. As I got to know my boyfriend my feelings just grew and grew. Now he's really important to me. I didn't expect it to happen like that.' **Leila, 18**

Compatibility

Feeling strongly about someone is pointless if you don't get on. A compatible couple is like-minded and well matched. It's more than having suited birth signs and sharing a love of football, it's about being attuned to one another in different ways.

How compatible are you? There are five areas of compatibility:

1. Physically – are you attracted to one another?
2. Emotionally – do you laugh, cry and get angry about the same things? Can you talk about your feelings?
3. Intellectual – are you on the same wavelength? Are you of similar intelligence?
4. Spiritual – do you share a faith? Do you have similar values, principles and goals?
5. Social – are you about the same age? Do you have similar interests and background?

You'll never achieve complete compatibility with another person, but some areas may be more important than others.

'I was really in love with a bloke a lot older than me and at first we had a great time. But it was hard because all his mates had cars, jobs and girlfriends their age. It just wasn't gonna work.'

Mandy, 18

'We were completely mad for each other, but we couldn't hold a conversation. She was a great lover, but rubbish to go out with.'   **Harry, 17**

As your relationship grows you may think about a future together. It's never easy to know when an investment in another person is a good or bad one, but a relationship reality check may give you some clues.

Relationship reality check

■ Do we bring out the best in one another?

■ Do we have relaxed, comfortable times together?

■ Do I feel I can be 'me' with her/him?

■ Do I like her/him as well as love her/him?

■ Do we respect and cherish one another?

■ Is our love happy and carefree more often than miserable and painful?

■ Do my friends and family like/approve of her/him? Do they have any valid reasons not to?

■ Am I going out with them because I like/love their company or because: they look good on my arm; it's great for my reputation; there's no-one else; no-one would expect it of me; they have a car/motorbike/house/job/credit card?

Making a commitment

When you're in love and enjoying a loving relationship, think about what makes it special. Love is the sensation that propels you towards one another, but other factors play an important part in making it real.

If you're unsure about the value of your relationship, look at the people around you who have good, solid partnerships and find out what makes them tick. Parents, relations, neighbours, friends, teachers and social workers can all provide role models. Don't be afraid to ask them the secret of their success. Just make sure they're happy to talk to you.

'If a girl's a mate first, a relationship stands a good chance. It's better to like someone a lot than to love them a lot and not like them at all!' **Joe, 17**

LIVING TOGETHER

Living together means sharing a life, not just a bed and kitchen. Move in together if you feel comfortable sharing intimate details of your lifestyle with your partner. Take a look at the checklist:

- How will you feel waking up beside her/him every morning?
- How will you feel fitting in with her/his lifestyle and routine?
- How are the everyday finances – including mortgage/rent, Council Tax, utility bills, shopping, car expenses etc. – going to be paid?
- How are you going to divide household chores – washing, ironing, shopping, cooking, cleaning etc.?

■ How will you feel about sharing your space?

■ How will you feel about her/his friends and family turning up?

■ How are you going to fit in your school/work routine and social life into your relationship?

■ How are you and your family going to feel about you leaving home?

■ How do you really feel about your girlfriend/boyfriend?

MARRIAGE

■ In 2002 there were 254,400 marriages in England and Wales. Of these, 150,200 were first marriages for both people and 46,700 were remarriages for both people.

■ The average age for first marriages in England and Wales in 2002 was 31 for men and 29 for women.

Source: www.statistics.gov.uk

Even though divorce is more common now than ever before, thousands of people get married and have happy, fulfilling unions that last into old age.

'Marriage is what I want in the future. I wouldn't feel bored with one person and I'm very loyal. That closeness and security must be wonderful.' **Marnie, 16**

Good reasons to get married:

- you're in love
- to make a commitment
- it's your culture
- to start a family
- to celebrate
- it's the right time.

Bad reasons to get married:

- to escape from home – marriage takes hard work and commitment, it's not an easy alternative to life at home
- to have sex – sex is important, but it can't sustain a relationship. You need more than sex to have a happy marriage

FACT BOX

Marriage and the law
Men and women can get married at 18 without their parents' consent. You can marry at 16 with the consent of both parents if they have parental responsibility for you. For those who are the subject of a care order the local trust must give consent in addition to parents. For those who are a ward of court the consent of the court is required. If consent to the marriage is refused by parents or the local authority, an application can be made to the court.

- to make your relationship secure – your relationship won't be more secure after marriage, it's just harder to separate
- fear of being alone – you can be very lonely in the wrong marriage. It's better to bet on future opportunities than get into a bad marriage
- one of you really wants to get married – both of you have to be committed to marriage
- you want a big wedding – a wedding is only a day; marriage is for life
- for the children – children benefit from living with two parents, but benefit most if you're happy. Marrying for a child's sake could make everyone unhappy.

CHAPTER SIX:

LOVERS
Sex and love

KISSING

Kissing is different from snogging. That peck on the cheek from a
whiskered aunt or the fashionista air kiss from an acquaintance, bears
no resemblance to a good snog.

That special toe-curling, hairs-on-the-back-of-the-neck sensation can
give a whole new insight into the way you feel and the way he/she
feels. It can indicate true love or it can feel like kissing a frog.
Passionate kissing can be instantly appreciated, but takes time to
master.

Tips on how to be a top-class kisser:
- energy and action don't make up for bad technique, so go gently
- move in slowly and explore, brushing lips against cheeks, eyes,
  forehead and nose
- work towards the mouth. Be sensitive and relax your lips, parting
  them slightly to gently brush them over hers/his
- feel the plumpness and shape of those lips and put slight pressure
  on them with yours, pouting out a kiss

- as her/his lips respond, softly move yours against them
- don't use tongues unless you know her/him well. Some people don't like tongues at all and French kissing is reserved for the throes of mad passion
- don't suck, don't slurp and don't press so hard your partner gets whiplash!

The secret is to *feel* your way around. Relax, lose yourself in the moment.

It's all very well mastering the techniques of first-class kissing, but if your partner hasn't got it sussed, you'll be disappointed. Telling someone they're a bad kisser is a no-no, but telling someone what you like (as kindly as possible) is OK.

TIP BOX

When you kiss you release dopamine, a chemical important for sexual arousal.

Kissing, like flirting, can be an end in itself, bringing two people closer together. However, it can also be a precursor to more intimate sexual exploration. Kissing other parts of the body is stimulating and can lead to orgasm. Whether you want to be kissed all over depends on whether you want it to become sexual rather than affectionate.

GOING FURTHER

The best sex is based on knowledge, understanding and respect with someone you care about. The first step to good sex is to know what you're dealing with. You need to feel comfortable with your body and confident about his/hers to give and receive pleasure. You may have learned about your body in biology, but what you've got, why it's there and what it does is fundamental to sexual experience.

Plumbing

Here's the low-down on the plumbing for boys and girls.

BOYS

The daily function of the penis is to eliminate urine, the body's liquid waste. Urine comes from the bladder and passes to the outside of the body through the urethra, which opens at the tip of the penis.

FACT BOX

An adult penis is usually 6–10 cm long when flaccid (soft) and 12–19 cm long erect (hard). The diameter is about 3–4 cm. Twelve-year-old boys typically have a penis that is 3–5 cm long when soft, and less than 8 cm when erect.

The other important function of the penis is to deliver sperm, made in the two testicles (balls) that hang below the penis. Blood fills the penis to make it erect, ready for penetration and ejaculation, when semen (the liquid containing sperm) is squirted into the vagina, to swim into the uterus (womb) and up the Fallopian tubes to fertilise the egg.

Just behind the penis is a sac – the scrotum – containing two testicles. These produce testosterone (the male hormone) and make sperm.

The sperm then travel around the testicles' chambers and tubes, combining with fluids to make semen.

Testicles are sensitive to temperature (they hang lower outside the body when warm and higher up when cold) and pressure. A knocked testicle can be very painful.

FACT BOX

Most boys/men have 3–15 contractions on ejaculation: each one lasts about a second and the first three are the biggest. Most men produce about a teaspoon of semen each time, containing up to 300 million sperm. Some boys/men can ejaculate several times a day. This changes, as a man gets older.

GIRLS

The opening to the vagina is one of three small holes, in between the urethral opening at the front which a girl urinates (wees) through and the anus at the back.

From the vaginal opening there is a tube called the vagina, which leads to the uterus (womb) via the cervix (opening to the womb). The vagina is about 7–10 cm long. It can stretch lengthways and sideways to fit any penis.

When a girl has a period the blood comes down her vagina. The hymen, a thin, elastic skin, partly covers the vaginal opening, but there's enough space for blood to get through. Sometimes the hymen breaks when a girl first has intercourse, but the hymen can also be broken during swimming or horse-riding.

The most important pleasure sex organ for girls is the clitoris. The clitoris sits above the vaginal and urethral openings and is connected to the labia minora. It's about the size of a pea. (If you want to look at your external genitals, lie on your back with your knees apart and put a mirror between your legs to reflect your vulva.)

The glans (the exposed part) is only a fifth of the whole organ. The glans is the only noticeable part of the erectile tissue, which pads the pubic bone. The size and shape vary: in some women it may be quite noticeable, in others it is small or hardly visible. The clitoris has no biological function. It's packed with nerve endings and can make sex very enjoyable, with stimulation leading to orgasm.

Orgasm

An orgasm is not the objective of sex. You can have a good time, feel aroused, sensual and intimate, and not have an orgasm.

Don't put pressure on achieving orgasm – it's a big turn off. Create a safe, comfortable and caring environment, then an orgasm may happen.

TIP BOX

What is an orgasm?
It's a climactic sensation, usually resulting from sexual stimulation, when:

- *the heart pumps faster and breathing becomes heavier*
- *hormones (endorphins and oxytocin) pump around brain and body, giving you a buzz*
- *blood pumps to the genitals, making them redder and swollen*
- *tension builds, eventually triggering a muscular spasm – the orgasm climax*
- *climax results in pelvic-floor muscles contracting between five and 15 times at 0.8-second intervals*
- *for some the sensation is a tingle, for others it's an all-over feeling.*

Men can come before they actually ejaculate. Ejaculating without climaxing is rare, but can also happen.

Men have a refractory period. This is the time it takes for a man to become stimulated again after ejaculation. Once a man comes, it will take ten minutes or more for him to become erect again. The younger the man, the less time it takes to recover. Women do not have a refractory period; they can become stimulated again almost instantly after orgasm.

Sexual exploration

There are many ways for you and your partner to express your sexual feelings. Sex doesn't just mean sexual intercourse – or having an orgasm. You can hold or cuddle your partner or kiss him or her in different ways. You can masturbate (wank) on your own or together. You can have oral sex with your partner.

DO YOU REALLY WANT TO HAVE SEX?

Whether to have sex can be a difficult decision, but you have to make that decision yourself. No-one else can decide for you and no-one should put pressure on you. Everyone has the right to say no to sex or any other behaviour that makes them uncomfortable at any time. It's your body and your choice, and it's important to wait until *you're* ready.

TIP BOX

Erogenous zones
- **feet** – *give your girlfriend/ boyfriend a foot massage*
- **knee pit** – *a stroked knee pit can be a real turn-on*
- **ears** – *gently kissing and sucking earlobes, combined with soft neck kissing, is lovely*
- **nape of the neck** – *the neck area has many nerve endings and responds to careful stimulation, especially as it's where tension collects in the muscles supporting the head*
- **head and hair** – *combing, brushing, washing or just running your fingers through your partner's hair can be tingly*
- **breasts** – *breasts are very sensitive and both girls and boys get pleasure from breast stroking, nipple pinching, kissing and sucking. Women tend to enjoy attention over the whole of the breast, while men enjoy specific nipple stimulation – especially when turned on*
- **G-spot** – *named after a male doctor (Grafenburg) and not really a spot but a region. In girls it lies behind the vaginal walls in*

the front, about one-third of the way up. The tissue here is soft and is most responsive when a girl is aroused. It can be touched or rubbed to climax: the G-spot orgasm. Boys have a sort of G-spot (the prostate gland), which can be reached by putting pressure on a similar area in the rectum. Externally, this is connected to the area between the scrotum and anus – also a pleasure hot spot.

Am I too young?

It is legal in England, Wales and Scotland for young men and women to have sex at 16. This also applies to sexual relationships between people of the same sex. In Northern Ireland the age of consent is 17, in Jersey it's 16, but 18 for gay men. In the Isle of Man, consensual male gay sex is legal only if you're over 21.

Am I ready for sex now?

Even if you are 16 and sex is legal, you may not feel adult enough. Friends shouldn't make you feel stupid for not wanting sex if it doesn't feel right. The age of consent is not a target to reach or beat.

Am I happy to have sex before marriage?

Don't be scared to stick to your beliefs. If you want to remain a virgin until you have a long-term commitment, stay strong and say 'no'.

Do I really want to have sex with this person?

Sex with the right person at the right time can be wonderful, but it's possible to have a loving relationship without having sex. Sex isn't the only way of showing how you feel.

What happens if I change my mind?

You have a right to say 'no' at any time, even if you have 'led someone on' because you thought you were ready.

If you're uncomfortable with what's happening, you should stop, or the experience will be bad for both of you and may make you feel negatively about sex. It's better to have no sex than bad sex.

You'll find it easier to say 'no' if you know how far you want to go. If there may be the opportunity for sex, think about it beforehand. Imagine what it's going to be like and how you may feel discussing it with your partner. If you can't talk about sex with someone – contraception and STIs, what you like and don't like, and how far you want to go – think about whether you should be having sex with them.

Sex – whether it's vaginal or anal penetration, or oral sex – is the closest you can get to someone. Think about how you may feel in an intimate situation.

MUTUAL MASTURBATION

Pleasuring your partner without having intercourse is a safe and exciting way to explore sensations. Mutual masturbation doesn't have to lead to penetration, ejaculation or orgasm. It can be a lovely way of relaxing your partner and getting closer.

Mutual masturbation gives you the opportunity to tell your partner what pleases you and to direct her/him to certain strokes, positions or erogenous zones. Don't be afraid to say what you like, but try not to be critical. Everyone has to learn and can improve with practice.

ORAL SEX

Oral sex can be enjoyable, whether receiving or giving, but not everyone finds it pleasurable. In some societies it's forbidden.

Stimulating sexual organs orally (with the mouth) mimics the action of the penis and vagina and can give greater pleasure than penetration. There are two types of oral sex – fellatio, when your mouth gives pleasure to his penis, and cunnilingus – when your mouth gives pleasure to her vulva.

FACT BOX

69 is when two people lie top-to-tail and give each other oral sex at the same time.

Giving oral sex involves lips, tongue, gums and teeth, in licking, nibbling, kissing and sucking motions. It's often combined with hand masturbation.

Different people enjoy different stimulation. In general, men tend to like stronger, definite and increasingly quickening stimulation, while women enjoy softer, slower strokes.

'I really like giving and receiving oral sex. I have the biggest orgasm when my boyfriend licks me. He goes mad with pleasure when I suck him. It's fun and I don't have to worry about getting pregnant.'
Maryam, 17

Oral sex is one way of enjoying your partner without fear of pregnancy, but because there's an exchange of body fluids, STIs can be transmitted orally. The risk of acquiring gonorrhoea or syphilis by oral sex is thought to be much higher than for HIV (see Chapter 7). You can protect yourself by using a dam (mouth shield) for cunnilingus and a male condom for fellatio, but these will not protect you against genital warts or herpes infection. If you have multiple partners, it's safer to get tested for STIs every six months. Testing is done in genito-urinary medicine (GUM) clinics.

SEXUAL INTERCOURSE

'Being grown-up about sex is treating yourself and other people with respect and not being afraid to ask for help if you need it or if you don't understand something.'
Source: fpa

Sexual intercourse is the ultimate step in sexual exploration. Once you've had penetrative sex you're no longer a virgin. You may feel it's important to keep your virginity until you are married or in a long-term relationship, or you may feel you need to lose your virginity by a certain age to keep up with your friends. Having sex is an adult act and, regardless of your peers or what you see on television, you need to be adult enough to handle it emotionally, as well as physically.

Under the influence

Having sex should be a decision you make with a clear head. Often teenagers have sex when they're drunk or have taken drugs, and regret it when they're sober. One of the effects of drink and some drugs is to make you less inhibited and to affect your judgement so you do things you wouldn't normally do. The problem with doing something under the influence is you have to come round – and reality hits. Waking up or sobering up with someone you've had sex with and can't face is a humiliating experience. It does nothing for your self-esteem – or your reputation. Bad sex, unprotected sex, or sex with the wrong person is just not worth having.

Ready for sexual intercourse?

If you and your partner feel ready for sex, there's no reason why you shouldn't have a good experience, but being ready means:

- feeling comfortable with your body and your feelings
- feeling comfortable about sex at a moral and religious level
- caring about your partner's well-being
- being able to talk to your partner about what you like and don't like
- knowing you can say 'no' – at any time
- agreeing with your partner on what contraception and protection you're using, and feeling comfortable with that choice
- knowing what your options are if you or your partner gets pregnant
- knowing what to do if you become infected with an STI.

Reasons not to have sexual intercourse

If you've planned to have sex, or someone has suggested you have sex, it's not a good idea if:

■ neither of you has protection

■ it goes against your morals or religion

■ you want to be in love

■ you want to wait until you're older

■ there's too much pressure

■ you don't like or trust your partner enough

■ you don't know what you're doing

■ you've got other things on your mind

■ you haven't had time to think about it properly

■ you don't feel turned on enough

■ the setting isn't right

■ someone may walk in

■ there are other people around

■ you don't feel well or sober

■ you've taken drugs.

The first time

Girls shouldn't panic if the first time is painful. If the hymen (the membrane that partially covers the entrance to the vagina) is still intact, it will be broken by sex. This is natural but can be a little painful and may bleed.

Sex may also be uncomfortable if the vagina isn't lubricated. This could be because the girl is not turned on enough or because she doesn't feel completely comfortable with penetration. A lubricant (like KY jelly) can help, but be careful what you use, as some products (such as Vaseline) can weaken condom rubber.

Sometimes penetration is difficult because a girl is worried and the vaginal muscles clench tight. This can often be solved with relaxation, increased arousal and increased gentle sexual experience over time. If you experience problems with muscle spasm, you may have a condition called vaginismus. Talk to your GP or a clinic counsellor for advice. If you have difficulties during penetration it may be your body's way of saying you don't want to go further.

FACT BOX

Globally, one in four people would have sex with a new partner in the first month
Almost one in six (15 per cent) would have sex on the first night.
Men (20 per cent) are more likely to have sex on the first night than women (7 per cent).

Anal sex

Penetrative anal sex is when a man puts his penis into a woman's anus. Legally, both people have to be at least 18, they both have to consent and they have to do it in a private place. Anal sex can be pleasurable for both people, but not everybody likes the idea of it and no-one should be forced to do it.

Anal sex has gained in popularity among young people because there's no risk of pregnancy. However, anal sex is the most effective way of transmitting STIs, including HIV (see Chapter 7). If you have anal sex, use a strong condom.

SEXUAL STEREOTYPES

In boys, high levels of testosterone can lead to a lot of sexual activity: boys grow up in a world where sexual behaviour is tolerated, and it only takes the biological trigger to start it off. Multiple partners for boys become a trophy rather than a stigma.

Girls, however, suffer from a double standard. They are not supposed to encourage boys – boys are supposed to make the moves, and girls to stay faithful to one partner. Even in the twenty-first century, girls are still stigmatised – called slapper, slag, and tart – if their sexual past becomes public knowledge.

This is an ancient attitude and it is changing – but slowly. You'll be aware of these sexual stereotypes and may have to face them at some time. However, knowing your own mind may help you to have the confidence to stand up for what you really think. It's difficult to be different, but sometimes the price is just too high to conform.

SEXUAL PARTNERS
Monogamy

To be monogamous means being with one partner exclusively. Serial monogamy means being with one person exclusively until the relationship ends and another monogamous partner is found. Monogamy works for people even if they're not having sex. When you get married, you make a promise to stay monogamous for life.

Monogamy is held in high esteem because it represents respect and commitment to one partner. It's also the healthiest sexual option. Having multiple sexual partners puts you at increased risk of STIs, including HIV (see Chapter 7), as well as cervical cancer, herpes and genital warts.

Casual sex

Casual sex means having sex with someone you're not having a relationship with, don't really know, or may never see again. In a casual encounter you concentrate on physical satisfaction without thinking too much about the other person.

Casual sex means there's no commitment, but it doesn't always mean there's no responsibility or care. Many people have casual encounters that are exciting and stimulating, and still feel good about themselves. Often, people have repeated casual sex because they fear intimacy. This kind of sex can make people feel worthless and confused about what they want from sex and relationships.

FACT BOX

Fewer than one in five people (17 per cent) say they would reduce their number of sexual partners to protect themselves against HIV and other STIs. **Source: Durex**

SEXUAL ABUSE AND ASSAULT

In legal terms, sexual abuse is when a person under the age of consent is pressured into any type of sexual contact they don't agree to. It can happen in different relationships and is about power. Abuse of any kind in any relationship is always wrong and is never the fault of the abused.

TIP BOX

Sexual abuse and the law
A new offence (under the Sexual Offences Act 2003) has been created to confront the 'grooming' of children. This is when an adult contacts, meets and forms a relationship with a child to sexually abuse her/him.
The 2003 Act recognises sexual abuse in situations where an adult has a position of trust or authority over a child, and in relationships defined by blood ties, adoption, fostering, marriage or common law partnerships.
The Act also deals with offences that involve consensual sexual activity with children aged 13 to 15. These offences criminalise both direct physical sexual activity and activity where no contact is made – such as forcing a child to watch a sexual act.

Abusers are often adults who have your trust or are in a position of care. Most child abuse takes place in the home and happens repeatedly. When sexual abuse happens within the family, it's called incest.

Sexual abuse relies on silence and the abuser is powerful only as long as the abuse is kept secret. Getting abuse out in the open reveals the

FACT BOX

Between 15 and 30 per cent of women have had an unwanted sexual experience in their childhood. Girls are 2–3 times more likely to be abused than boys. Sexual abuse happens to young people of all ages and from all cultures.

abuser (stopping the abuse) and helps the abused person start to heal. Children who speak up are far more likely to recover from their experiences enough to have safe, loving, long-term relationships later in life.

TIP BOX

If anyone touches you, talks dirty to you, asks you to watch them in a sexual act or in any way makes you feel uncomfortable with their behaviour:
- *say NO – firmly*
- *tell them to STOP what they are doing*
- *tell them to go away immediately*
- *tell them you'll TELL someone what's happened*
- *try to find a way to get away first, if you feel unsafe.*

If you've been abused, you can tell your teacher, social worker, youth leader, Connexions adviser, doctor, priest, imam or rabbi – or contact one of the organisations in Helpful Organisations. If you look under 'rape' in the Yellow Pages you'll find local numbers to call.

Sexual assault

Sexual assault is when someone does something sexual you haven't consented to. It is usually an attack or a one-off act. It's a crime and should be reported.

FACT BOX	*Indecent assault, rape and the law*
	Indecent assault can be committed by a man or woman and is based on the assault being intentionally indecent.

Rape is the physical act of having sexual intercourse (vaginal or anal) with a man or woman without their consent. A man (aged over 14) commits rape if he has unlawful sexual intercourse with a person who at the time does not consent to it, and if at that time he knows the person does not consent to it.

Under the Sexual Offences Act 2003 there is a new clause covering 'date rape', which says that anyone having sex with someone who is unconscious or drugged can be accused of rape, and anyone drugging someone can be accused of intent to rape.

CHAPTER SEVEN:

SEXPERTS
How to be a sexpert

A sexpert knows how to have and give pleasure responsibly, wisely, and with feeling. You need to know about the serious side of sex as well as the fun side. That may sound boring, but the effects of bad sex, forced sex and irresponsible sex can be tragic and lifelong.

'Getting a girl pregnant is so scary. Pregnancy is one of the big worries for teenagers. I carry johnnies around with me all the time. I'm taking no chances!'

Alex, 16

Often the opportunity for sex arrives before you know enough to act sensibly. That's why it's worth reading this chapter, even if you don't think you'll be having sex yet.

The great thing about sex is that it's something everyone can do at some point in their lives, so there are many people with sexual experiences you can relate to. But don't believe everyone who says they're doing it. Research shows only three out of ten boys and girls under 16 have had sex. Seventy per cent haven't.

Because everyone can do it, everyone thinks they're a sexpert, which can be a problem when you need straight answers to sex questions. If you need facts, go to good organisations and Internet sites (see Helpful Organisations) or ask someone you trust.

Sex myths

ALL the statements below are FALSE.

▧ You won't get pregnant having sex standing up, or in water.
No: a girl can get pregnant in any position, anywhere.

▧ You won't get pregnant the first time you have sex.
No: a girl can get pregnant any and every time, even before she's had her first period.

▧ You won't get pregnant during your period.
No: a girl is only *less* likely to get pregnant during her period, as she is most fertile in the middle of her cycle.

▧ A girl won't get pregnant unless she has an orgasm.
No: she doesn't need to come to get pregnant.

▧ You won't get pregnant if he withdraws just before ejaculating (coming).
No: a girl can still get pregnant because there are sperm in the pre-cum (semen) a boy dribbles out when he's very turned on.

▧ Kissing isn't fun unless it leads to sex.
No: having a good snog doesn't have to be a run-up to sex.

▧ Boys have to have sex if they get aroused.
No: boys get aroused all the time. If they had sex that often, they'd never stop doing it!

- You don't really love someone if you don't want to have sex with them.
  No: love isn't just about sex, it's about trust, honesty and respect. If you have those in your relationship, your girl/boyfriend won't push you to have sex with him/her if you don't want to.

- Girls are born with a lifetime supply of eggs.
  No: women have a limited number of eggs in their ovaries. They usually run out during the menopause.

- If boys masturbate a lot they eventually stop producing sperm.
  No: boys continually produce sperm. At some points during the day or night production may be lower but there are millions in their testicles.

PROTECTION SELECTION

FACT BOX

You can get free and confidential contraception and sexual health advice from the doctor, clinics and young people's services, even if you are under 16.

It's easy to get carried away on a wave of lust. Although sex can be spontaneous and passionate, some things need to be sorted out before the kissing starts.

Contraception and protection may be awkward and boring but it's more awkward and boring getting pregnant or catching a sexually transmitted disease. Making love knowing you've done everything to stay healthy makes sex more relaxed and enjoyable.

FACT BOX

According to Marie Stopes research in 2002, over half of 11–15-year-olds don't know condoms can prevent HIV and STI transmission; and almost a tenth think injectable contraception and intra-uterine devices (IUDs) offer protection against HIV and STIs — they don't.

Finding out what will work best for you and your partner can be tricky, but there are reliable (and accessible) methods available to young people.

	CHEMICAL	CHEMICAL	CHEMICAL	CHEMICAL
CONTRACEPTIVE METHODS	Combined pill	Progestogen only pill	Contraceptive patch	Injectable contraceptive
How well does it work?	Over 99% effective if taken properly	99% effective if taken properly	Over 99% effective if used properly	Over 99% effective
Advantages?	Reduces heavy and painful period symptoms. Controls timing of periods. Protects against cancer of ovary and womb. Doesn't affect love-making. No-one need know you are taking it	For women who cannot take the combined pill	Only have to replace the patch once a week	Depro-Provera lasts for 12 weeks, Noristerat lasts for 8 weeks

	CHEMICAL	CHEMICAL	CHEMICAL	CHEMICAL
Disadvantages?	You have to remember to take it every day. Side-effects such as headaches, nausea. Rare serious side-effects like blood clots and breast and cervical cancer. Doesn't protect against STIs such as chlamydia and HIV	You have to remember to take the pill every day. Can make periods irregular with breakthrough bleeding. Doesn't protect against STIs such as chlamydia and HIV	Side-effects such as headaches, nausea. Rare serious side-effects like blood clots and breast and cervical cancer. Doesn't protect against STIs such as chlamydia and HIV	Can make periods irregular or stop altogether. Some weight gain and mood changes

	BARRIER	BARRIER	INTERNAL	INTERNAL
CONTRACEPTIVE METHODS	Condoms	Cap and diaphragm (and spermicide)	IUD (intra-uterine device)	IUS (intra-uterine system)
How well does it work?	Male condom 98%, female condom 95% effective if both used properly	90–96% effective if used properly	Over 98% effective	Over 99% effective
Advantages?	Freely available – free from family planning and sexual health clinics, sold widely. Gives protection against STIs and cancer of the cervix.	Can be put in any time before sex. Gives some protection against STIs.	Works for 3–8 years.	Works for at least 3 years. Gap between periods is shorter, but periods are lighter.
Disadvantages?	Requires careful use and confidence. May break or slip off. Lessens sensation. Can interrupt love-making	Requires careful use. Can be messy. Extra spermicide needed for repeated sex	Periods may be heavier, longer and more painful. Doesn't protect against STIs – like chlamydia and HIV	Light bleeding for first six weeks to three months. Some side-effects like acne, mood changes and tender breasts. Doesn't protect against STIs

	BARRIER	BARRIER	INTERNAL	INTERNAL
Most suitable for?	Everyone!	Women who do not get on with the pill and who are comfortable with touching themselves internally	Older women and those who have been pregnant	Older women and those who have been pregnant

The most popular contraception methods for teenagers are the pill (taken by girls) and the condom (worn by boys). There are advantages and disadvantages to each, but it's important to remember that **the condom is the only method that offers protection, not just from unplanned pregnancy, but from sexually transmitted infections (STIs) including HIV**.

FACT BOX

Over half of women aged 18–19 in Great Britain use the pill. Forty-two per cent of female teenagers aged 16–17 were using the pill in 2001–2002 (an increase from 18% in 2000).
Source: Office for National Statistics

TIP BOX

Contraception and the law Doctors can provide contraceptive advice and treatment (without parental consent) to under-16s providing they believe it's in the child's best medical interests and the patient is able to give informed consent. Girls aged 16 or over can buy the morning-after pill over the counter from pharmacies, but those under 16 have to go to their GP, family planning clinic, NHS walk-in clinic or advisory centre (e.g. Brook, Marie Stopes).

Confidentiality
Health workers (doctors and nurses) have a duty to keep information about you private (unless they suspect a patient is being seriously hurt or in danger). If you are under 16, health workers will keep your consultation confidential unless they decide you are not mature enough to make decisions about treatment. This would normally be discussed with you first.

Parents can see their children's records if the young person gives permission. Permission can be refused if the information in the records was given on the assumption that it would not be disclosed.

'Condoms are a bit of a pain sometimes, but they protect you from everything, so it's worth it. You just get used to them.'

Maryam, 17

TIP BOX

How to put on a condom

1. *Open the individual condom sachet carefully, making sure you don't tear the condom – have it open and ready beforehand if you know you're about to have sex.*

2. *Make sure the penis is erect (hard).*

3. *Take out the condom and place it over the penis with the reservoir (nipple) end over the top of the penis head.*

4. *Pinch the reservoir and start to unroll the condom over the penis head (if there's no reservoir, pinch the end carefully to make room for the sperm).*

5. *Using both hands, unravel the condom over the head, being careful not to catch your nails in the condom.*

6 *If the condom is difficult to unravel, it may be inside out. Take off the condom and check which way it is rolled, then start again.*

7 *If the penis is uncircumcised, gently pull back the foreskin and carefully unroll the condom over the widest part.*

8 *Unroll the condom all the way to the base of the penis, pulling it down gently as far as it will go.*

9 *Smooth out any air bubbles.*

10 *As soon as the boy has ejaculated, take the penis out of the vagina, anus or mouth, making sure the condom is held at the base. If you wait until the penis is soft, semen can spill out.*

11 *Still holding the base, slip the penis out of the condom and throw the condom in a bin.*

The biggest complaint about the male condom is that it interrupts foreplay and delays intercourse – it's something you have to remember, usually at the last minute. But the condom can become an intrinsic part of sex. It's especially pleasurable for a boy if a girl puts on the condom while masturbating him. It's easier (and adds to the sensation) if you use a lubricant like KY jelly.

FACT BOX

If you use a spermicide every time you have sex, you can increase a condom's effectiveness to almost 100 per cent.

Girls can take the lead with condoms – buying them, applying them and making sure the boy knows it's important to use one. Although it's great to find a method of protection a boy can organise, it's not just down to boys to get condoms. A girl who carries condoms when she may have sex is being sensible, not a slag.

Be clever with condoms

■ Always use condoms whenever you have vaginal or anal sex (and if possible use un-lubricated condoms or mouth shields when giving oral sex).

■ Choose condoms that are in date, undamaged and have the European standard mark.

■ Store them away from heat – preferably not in a wallet or back pocket.

■ Use a condom once only!

■ Choose condoms with reservoir tips to hold the semen, and always squeeze out the air from the tip as you put it on.

■ If the condom splits, replace it immediately with a new one and use emergency contraception if necessary.

■ Don't be put off if the condom you are using feels too tight or too short: choose another brand or type. Experiment with what feels comfortable and gives (both of you) the most pleasure.

■ Dispose of condoms considerately – not down the loo or in a public place.

EMERGENCY CONTRACEPTION

Two types of contraception can be used after unprotected sex:

■ the emergency pill (the morning-after pill) must be started within three days (72 hours) of sexual intercourse. The earlier they are taken, the more effective they become

■ an IUD (intra-uterine device) must be fitted within five days of sexual intercourse.

You can get emergency contraception free from: a doctor or nurse at your local surgery; a family planning clinic; a young people's clinic (such as Brook); genito-urinary medicine (GUM) clinics in large hospitals; or sexual health clinics (e.g. Marie Stopes). You can buy emergency contraception over the counter from pharmacies if you are 16 or over.

SEXUALLY TRANSMITTED INFECTIONS

In the 1980s the campaign to prevent the spread of AIDS made everyone aware of safe sex issues, but since then condom use has declined – especially among young people. STIs are on the increase among young heterosexuals.

FACT BOX

STIs (sexually transmitted infections) are also known as STDs (sexually transmitted diseases) and they used to be called VD (venereal disease) – named after Venus, the goddess of love.

THE LOWDOWN ON STIs

STIs	CHLAMYDIA	PELVIC INFLAMMATORY DISEASE (PID)	GONORRHOEA	SYPHILIS
What is it?	A bacterium (Chlamydia trachomatis) can affect genitals and cervix (entrance to the womb), urethra (tube where urine comes out), rectum (back passage), throat and eyes	Inflammation and infection of the uterus and Fallopian tubes caused by bacteria – often Chlamydia	A bacterium (Gonococcus) infecting genitals, urethra, rectum and throat. Sometimes called 'the clap'	A disease caused by a bacterium. It's quite rare in the UK but common elsewhere and becoming common in America. Sometimes called 'the pox'.
What are the symptoms in women?	Frequently there aren't any, but an unusual discharge, pelvic aches during intercourse, and a slight temperature can indicate infection	An unusual discharge, irregular periods, lower pelvic pain and increased temperature. PID can be acute (one painful bout) or chronic (building up over time)	Up to 50% of women have no symptoms at all. Symptoms can include unusual discharge from the vagina, pain when peeing, a sore rectum and sore throat	There may be no symptoms. Painless round sores may appear on the vagina or vulva 2–3 weeks after infection. These can last for 6 weeks. A painless, non-irritating rash may follow, spreading all over the body, including palms of hands and soles of feet. After this stage there may be no symptoms for years

STIs	CHLAMYDIA	PELVIC INFLAMMATORY DISEASE (PID)	GONORRHOEA	SYPHILIS
What are the symptoms in men?	The most common cause of inflammation in the testicles and sperm-carrying tubes (epididymides). It causes pain, swelling and redness in the scrotum. May trigger joint inflammation	None	Only about 10% of men experience symptoms – unusual discharge from the penis, pain when peeing, a sore rectum and sore throat	There may be no symptoms. Painless round sores may appear on the penis 2–3 weeks after infection. These can last for 6 weeks. A painless, non-irritating rash may follow, spreading all over the body, including palms of hands and soles of feet. After this stage there may be no symptoms for years
What if it's untreated?	It can lead to PID and can damage follicles which pass the egg from the ovary to the Fallopian tube, making it difficult to conceive. It can increase risk of future ectopic pregnancy – which can be life-threatening	Can result in permanent damage to the Fallopian tubes, and infertility or increased risk of future ectopic pregnancy – which can be life-threatening	It can spread throughout reproductive organs causing serious long-term health problems, and reduced fertility or infertility in both men and women	It can have very serious effects on the brain and nervous system leading to insanity, followed by death. Heart, bones, liver and skin can all be affected. A pregnant woman can pass it on to her unborn baby
What's the treatment?	Chlamydia is the most common treatable STI and a one-off antibiotic prescription clears it up quickly	A strong, one-off antibiotic treatment clears it up quickly	Early treatment with antibiotics is effective. A follow-up test 3–7 days after treatment ensures it worked	Penicillin is an effective cure. Blood tests for syphilis are offered in most GUM clinics

STIs	CHLAMYDIA	PELVIC INFLAMMATORY DISEASE (PID)	GONORRHOEA	SYPHILIS
What's the prevention?	Safer sex using a condom. But some bacteria can be passed on by genital contact without penetration. If you have suspicions, talk to your GP or go to a GUM clinic	Safer sex using a condom. If you have suspicions, talk to your GP or go to a GUM clinic	Safer sex using a condom. If you have suspicions, talk to your GP or go to a GUM clinic	Safer sex using a condom. If you have suspicions, talk to your GP or go to a GUM clinic

STIS	GENITAL WARTS	GENITAL HERPES	HEPATITIS A, B, C
What is it?	An extremely contagious virus in the Human Papillomavirus (HPV) family. They look like ordinary warts and infect external genitals and anus. These develop between 3 weeks and 1 year after infection	A virus. Two types of herpes virus can affect the genitals; one also affects the mouth	Three different types of virus, all attack the liver. A – carried in faeces; B – carried in blood and body fluids through kissing, vaginal, anal and oral sex; C – carried in blood, semen and vaginal fluids
What are the symptoms in women?	Genital warts are often so small they can't be seen. They can be itchy and painful – especially inside the vagina	Most women are infected during intercourse and develop herpes on the vulva. Sores also appear on the clitoris, cervix, buttocks, thighs, belly button, and inside the anus and vagina. Many women have an increase in vaginal discharge	A – some don't have symptoms, others feel fluey 2–6 weeks after infection. Faeces turn pale and urine darkens. The next stage is jaundice. B – as below. C – symptoms develop 10–15 years after infection. Symptoms vary, including fatigue, nausea, vomiting, fever, diarrhoea and jaundice

STIS	GENITAL WARTS	GENITAL HERPES	HEPATITIS A, B, C
What are the symptoms in men?	Genital warts are often so small they can't be seen. They can be itchy and painful	Sores develop on the penis head and shaft, scrotum, buttocks, thighs and anus	A – as above. B – some don't have symptoms, but may experience fatigue, sore throat, headache, diarrhoea, poor appetite, aching muscles, upset stomach and fever 6 weeks– 6 months after infection. Faeces may turn pale and urine may darken. The next stage is jaundice. C – as above
What if it's untreated?	The risk of re-infection is very high, so they can appear all over your body. Certain types of HPV can cause pre-cancer and cancer	The risk of re-infection is very high, so the sores can appear all over your body. Herpes in the eye can lead to blindness. In pregnancy herpes can lead to miscarriage or complications	A – rarely leads to serious complications. B – can result in liver failure, liver cancer and death. C – most people have Hep C for the rest of their lives. It causes serious liver damage in a quarter of sufferers

FACT BOX

Chlamydia is the most common preventable cause of infertility in women. If you have chlamydia there's a good chance you also have gonorrhoea, and vice versa.

STIS	GENITAL WARTS	GENITAL HERPES	HEPATITIS A, B, C
What's the treatment?	There's no cure for genital warts. Once the virus is present, you're infected for life. They can be removed individually. There's a high risk of re-infection. Sometimes they go away as the immune systems fights back	There's no cure for herpes. Once the virus is present, you are infected for life. Treatment is based on keeping outbreaks to a minimum and making them manageable	A – no specific test for Hep A. The illness goes away naturally. Plenty of rest, no stress and a good diet all help the immune system to recover. B – plenty of rest, no stress, drugs or alcohol, and a good diet help the immune system. C – drug treatment is not effective for everyone. No alcohol
What's the prevention?	HPV can be caught by skin contact, through mutual masturbation, oral, anal and vaginal sex	Having a strong immune system gives the best protection against infection. Using a condom will protect against infectious sores on the penis and in the vagina. Sores on other areas should not be touched. Once infected, too much sun can activate the virus	A – a safe effective vaccine. Wash hands thoroughly after going to the toilet and sexual acts involving the anus. Wear a condom for anal sex. B – a safe vaccine effective 95% of the time. Practise safe sex. Don't get close to anyone jaundiced. Don't share razors, needles or toothbrushes. C – no vaccine. Practise safe sex. Don't get close to anyone jaundiced. Don't share razors, needles, or toothbrushes

TIP BOX

How do you get infected?
- *most commonly, through unprotected vaginal or anal intercourse*
- *you can get herpes and some other infections through oral sex*
- *some infections are passed through genital contact without penetration*
- *infections can be passed on during intercourse even if the boy withdraws, because pre-cum is released before ejaculation.*

FACT BOX

More than half a million diagnoses of sexually transmitted infections (STIs) were made in UK specialist sexual health clinics in 2000 – a third more than in 1995. **Source: fpa**

Symptom watch

General genito-urinary symptoms indicate something is wrong. You may have similar symptoms for different conditions. **If you are a boy and have**: pain when peeing, difficulty peeing, frequent peeing, a discharge (thick, watery, yellow, white or smelly) or sore testicles, a sore penis or pain on penetration, get medical advice.

If you are girl and have: pain when peeing, difficulty peeing, frequent peeing, an unusual discharge (thick, watery, yellow, white or smelly), low belly ache, pelvic pain on one side, breakthrough bleeding between periods, unusually heavy periods, periods with dark brown (not bright red) blood, bleeding after intercourse, irregular periods, internal or external pain or discomfort during sex or sore or tender genitals, get medical advice.

FACT BOX

Women catch STIs more easily than men. The vagina has a larger area of mucous membrane (which can be infected) than the penis, which is mostly skin.

Symptoms appear two to 14 days after infection for most of the above conditions, but they can incubate for up to four weeks. Because STIs can be passed on so easily, it's a good idea to have regular checks if you are sexually active. Your local GUM clinic or your GP will advise you. If you are infected, you are also infectious, so tell your recent sexual partner (or partners) so they can get treatment. It's not easy, but it's sensible and considerate.

HIV INFECTION AND AIDS

HIV (human immunodeficiency virus) lives in blood cells and attacks the body's natural immune defences. It can lead to AIDS (acquired immune deficiency syndrome). AIDS is not a disease, it's a collection of illnesses and conditions that affect the body when its immune system is attacked by HIV. Many people with HIV remain healthy for decades and don't develop AIDS.

FACT BOX

Five million people worldwide were newly infected with HIV in 2002.
Source: World Health Organization

Essential HIV facts

▓ HIV is transmitted through blood and blood products, vaginal fluids and semen.

▓ It is difficult to transmit as it has to get into the bloodstream – through a cut or graze, via a needle or infected transfusion, or from mother to child in the womb and when breastfeeding.

▓ Since 1994, hospital blood products in Britain have been screened against HIV contamination.

▓ Sexually transmitted HIV occurs when infected vaginal fluid or semen gets into a partner's bloodstream through cuts or grazes in the mouth, vagina, anus or on the penis. Anal sex carries the highest risk as the anus doesn't expand like the vagina and penetration can cause abrasions that become infection routes.

Precautions against HIV

▓ Practise safe sex every time you have intercourse.

▓ Use an extra strong condom if you have anal sex.

▓ Use an unlubricated condom or mouth shield when having oral sex.

▓ Never pick up used condoms or used needles/syringes.

▓ You can't become HIV positive by sharing cups, toothbrushes or clothes, or through mouth-to-mouth kissing, cuddling or holding hands. The virus can only live in the bloodstream; it won't survive outside the body.

▓ You can't tell if someone has HIV or AIDS.

FACT BOX

In 2001–2002 the partners of one in five women were using the male condom, sometimes in addition to another form of contraception. **Source: Durex**

THE SMEAR TEST

A cervical smear (Pap test) tests cells on a girl's cervix (entrance to the womb). These are examined for signs of cancer or pre-cancer. Treatment at an early stage (by removing the cells) is very successful, which is why the NHS tests all sexually active women from the age of 25, every three years. Women under this age can request a smear test from their GP or GUM clinic. A girl who sees her doctor for contraceptive advice or has an STI will usually be recommended for a smear.

Cancer of the cervix is caused by the human papilloma viruses (HPVs) which are a group of different viruses, including ones that cause genital warts. The virus may not cause any symptoms and most HPV infections are fought off by your immune system. However, an HPV virus can show up years after infection and lead to cervical cancer.

The more sexual partners you have, the more exposed you are to STIs, including HPV. You should do everything you can to limit the possibility of HPV infection (by practising safer sex) and girls should go for regular cervical smears.

The smear is simple and painless. A girl lies down with her legs open and a speculum is inserted into the vagina to keep the vaginal walls apart. It may feel cold and slightly uncomfortable. The more relaxed you are, the easier it is. A sample is taken from your cervix on a spatula or brush and sent off for analysis. If there are any queries about the test or if any abnormal cells are found, you'll be contacted immediately.

How to have a happy sex life

■ DO talk and DO listen – get advice from parents, your GP or a clinic if you have queries.

■ DO think carefully before you have sex. The only sure way to prevent STIs or unplanned pregnancy is NOT to have sex. Your chances of getting STIs and cancer of the cervix are reduced if you stick to one partner and have protected sex.

■ DON'T have sex if you don't want to.

■ DO use contraception – always use a reliable method such as condoms or the pill.

■ DO use a condom – even if she's on the pill. Condoms protect against STIs like chlamydia, gonorrhoea and HIV.

■ DO learn how to put on a condom – if it's not put on properly, it won't work.

■ DO keep condoms with you.

- DON'T think sex is only vaginal penetration – there are many fun things you can do that don't risk pregnancy or infection (see Chapter 6).

- DON'T expect sex to be fantastic every time – sex the first time, or with a new partner, can be disappointing. As you learn more about sex and each other, it will improve.

- DON'T expect to orgasm every time, or at the same time. Women don't always orgasm (especially with penetration alone) and he may come quickly or not at all.

- DON'T lie back and think of England – great sex is all about giving and receiving.

CHAPTER EIGHT:

PREGNANCY
Are you pregnant?

Part of being ready for sex is deciding on and organising contraception (see Chapters 6 and 7), but pregnancy is a real risk:

- if the condom split
- if he ejaculated close to her vagina
- if she forgot to take the pill
- if she had a stomach upset or sickness and forgot to use additional contraception to the pill
- if both were drunk and didn't use anything at all
- if she had intercourse without consent (unwillingly).

FACT BOX

Every year about 100,000 teenage girls become pregnant in the UK.

Source: fpa, 2003

If you know you've had unprotected sex, emergency contraception is available within 120 hours (IUD) and 72 hours (the emergency contraceptive pill) of intercourse. If you're over 16 you can buy the pill from a pharmacy, but younger girls have to get medical advice first. It's best to see your GP or an adviser at your local family planning clinic.

Conception facts

■ Each testicle makes about 200 million sperm a day (2,000 per second) but only one sperm is needed to fertilise an egg.

■ There are about 2,000 sperm in a drop of semen the size of a pinhead.

■ A girl's ovum (egg) can be fertilised by sperm ejaculated up to seven days before.

■ The egg only lives for 12–24 hours.

■ Conception is most likely during ovulation (when the egg is released into the Fallopian tube). This occurs midway through the menstrual cycle – 12–16 days **before** the start of the **next** period.

■ On average, it takes a couple 3–6 months to conceive if they have regular, unprotected intercourse.

AM I PREGNANT?

Early signs of pregnancy:

■ missing a period

■ a shorter, lighter period than before

■ increased peeing

■ tender breasts or 'buzzing' nipples

■ crampy period-type pains

■ feeling sick and going off some food and drink

FACT BOX

One in every ten babies in England is born to a teenage mother. Girls from the poorest backgrounds are ten times more likely to become teenage mothers than girls from professional backgrounds.

Source: Department of Health

- a metallic taste when eating and drinking
- feeling very tired and wanting to sleep during the day
- feeling bloated.

If you think you may be pregnant, the only way to tell for sure is to take a pregnancy test. Tests carried out (free) by your doctor, GUM clinic or family planning clinic may have to be done after the date your period is due and may take a couple of days to come back. Most tests bought from a pharmacy can be used from the day your period is due (28 days after the date of your last period) and some specific over-the-counter tests can be used accurately a few days before. Some test packs are more expensive but offer two tests so you can make doubly sure of your result. Read the packet carefully and always follow the instructions.

If you think you're pregnant, talk it over with someone you trust. Try to involve a parent. You may feel you can't easily approach them, but most parents are more caring than judgemental. Their support and practical advice may help you make a decision about the future. Remember, if you're pregnant, the ultimate decision is yours alone, but it takes two to make a baby and the father should at least know what you're planning.

There are three main options:
- birth and motherhood
- birth and adoption
- termination (abortion).

Contact your GP or a family planning clinic as soon as you know you're pregnant. It's important to find out about your choices, so ask the professionals questions and if you can, look up information on reputable websites (see Helpful Organisations). There will be a lot to think about, so try to make a list of what's important.

FACT BOX

The UK has the highest teenage birth and abortion rates in Western Europe **Source: UNICEF**

When you're wondering what to do, think about the impact your decision will have. Consider your life, your baby's life, the father's life and your family's life – now and in the future. It's your decision, but your choice will affect other people's lives as well as yours.

'I think it's cruel for the child as well as for the mother to bring up an unwanted child. A baby should be wanted, loved and properly cared for. It's forever. You never stop being a parent. It's all right having a cute baby to show off, but what about that lifelong responsibility?' **Gee, 18**

There are a few questions you need to ask yourself:

- what's important to me now?
- what will be important to me in the future?
- how will I feel about making that decision?
- can I imagine myself coping and being happy in the future having made that decision?
- how will it affect my life in five, ten, 20 years' time?
- how will it affect my relationship with my family, friends, the baby's father?
- will my friends and family support me in my decision?
- will I be able to cope on my own?

BECKY'S STORY

'I had my son when I was 19. I'd been with his father three years and we planned it. I was young but there are advantages – you've loads of energy, you just get on with things, and grandparents are younger. My mum has helped a lot. It would have been difficult without her, and my boyfriend's a really good dad. I don't feel I've missed out, I've really enjoyed it.' **Becky, 27**

Taking advice from people who know the reality of those choices (parents, doctors, nurses, teachers, counsellors, social workers, youth advisers) is important, but only you can make the final decision. No girl should be forced to have an abortion, or a child, if it's not right for her, just as no boy should be pressured into becoming a father or husband if he isn't willing and ready to take on that role.

BECOMING A PARENT

Parenthood can be enriching and rewarding and most parents would say they wouldn't have missed out on being one. But becoming a parent when you've made the decision in advance, when you feel mature, secure and confident enough to have a child, is very different from accidentally becoming a prospective mother or father.

'People look at me on the bus as if to say, "she's just a teenager, how can she love her child?" But I do, just as much as any other mum. I love her and I look after her. I'd do anything for her.' **Lisa, 17**

Your child will be reliant on you until at least the age you are now. Most responsibility inevitably lies with the mum. Teenage fathers may be excited about being a dad and may want to create a family unit, but many find it difficult to imagine being depended on forever.

'When my girlfriend got pregnant I didn't have any strong feelings about my child. I was happy to go along with anything she wanted. After all, it's her body, her life, her future, isn't it?' **James, 15**

Funding a baby is a big issue. By the time you're 16, you will have cost almost £100,000 to bring up. If a girl can rely on family help with the child, it improves her chances of returning to education and training for a job or career. But many families may need additional help from Social Services to support an extended family. Child care and tax credits are available for young mothers who work a minimum of 16 hours a week.

ABORTION

FACT BOX

Over half of conceptions in girls aged under 16 were terminated in 2000.
Source: Office for National Statistics

Terminating a pregnancy is a big decision and an extremely difficult one to make, no matter what age you are.

What happens if I want an abortion?

The first step is to go to your doctor or clinic to make sure you are pregnant and discuss your decision. If you are under 16 and you want an abortion, you will be advised to tell a parent or another adult close to you.

Medical staff will be able to tell how many weeks pregnant you are by a pelvic examination or ultrasound (a scan). If you have an idea of when you may have got pregnant, tell the doctor. It's simple to work out how many weeks gone you are by starting at the first day of your last period and counting the weeks since then. You'll be more than four weeks, as you won't know you're pregnant until you've missed your first period.

If you're going to have an abortion, the earlier the better, so go to your GP, family planning or sexual health clinic as soon as you think you're pregnant.

TIP BOX

Abortion and the law
The 1967 Abortion Act (UK) says abortion is legal up to the 24th week of pregnancy, and most hospitals and clinics won't consider termination beyond 18–20 weeks. However, if there is a risk to the woman's life or health or if there are serious foetal abnormalities, there is no time limit. (The 1967 Act does not extend to Northern Ireland.)

A girl under 16 may be able to have an abortion without her parents' approval. The doctors have to believe that she understands the decision and that it is in her best interests to have an abortion without parental consent. If a girl under 16 doesn't want an abortion, she can't be forced to have one.

By law, two doctors need to agree to the abortion. If they believe there is a serious risk to the girl's mental or physical health if she continues with the pregnancy, they will agree to an abortion. The doctor also considers social circumstances (your situation at home, school, work and whether you have any support).

The doctor will send a termination request to the nearest hospital or clinic and an appointment will be made for you. Many hospitals now have specialist early pregnancy clinics. Marie Stopes and British Pregnancy Advisory Service both have clinics around the UK. (See Helpful Organisations.)

MANDY'S STORY

'I had an early abortion a few years ago. It was very straightforward and it was the right decision at the time. I was studying, I was in debt, I had no home of my own and a long time to go before I could support myself, let alone anyone else. The father was OK about the pregnancy but he wasn't that interested and I didn't want to be with him. I have no regrets, but each year at the time my baby would have been born, I think about her or him and have a cry.'

Mandy, 23

There are two types of early abortion used in the UK:

■ A medical termination (abortion pill) is like a natural miscarriage and is performed up to nine weeks. The girl is given two different drugs. The first (mifepristone) is taken at the hospital or clinic. It's an anti-progesterone drug, which stops the pregnancy. After 48 hours, she returns and is given prostaglandin. The termination usually occurs 4–6 hours later. This method is not available at all hospitals or clinics.

■ A surgical termination (early abortion) is performed from seven to 15 weeks. It takes about ten minutes and is done under local or general anaesthetic. The contents of the uterus are removed through the cervix and vagina by suction.

These procedures don't usually require an overnight stay.

There are three types of later abortion:

■ Medical induction is performed at over 12 weeks. The process is similar to medical termination but it's usual to stay overnight.

■ Surgical dilation and evacuation (D&E) takes about 20 minutes and is performed under general anaesthetic from about 15 weeks. Suction and forceps remove the content of the uterus. This sometimes requires an overnight stay.

■ Abortions over 20 weeks are rare but are performed by either the two-stage procedure (similar to D&E) or medical induction (which causes a labour similar to late miscarriage). These are carried out under general anaesthetic, with one or two nights' stay in hospital.

It's normal to experience some pain during these procedures and mild (period-type) pain for the first couple of days after a termination. This can be reduced by normal pain-killers like ibuprofen and paracetamol.

Abortion carries some risk of pelvic inflammatory disease (PID – see Chapter 7) when bacteria enter the uterus, leading to infection and inflammation. Symptoms are an unusual discharge, lower tummy pain and fever. PID can be treated effectively with a high-dose antibiotic.

ADOPTION

Adoption of babies happens less frequently these days: most girls who continue with a pregnancy keep the baby.

However, adoption can give a baby the opportunity to grow up in a loving family. It's a heart-rending decision that will stay with you forever, so you must be 100 per cent sure you want to give up your baby. Think about how you will feel in the future if you go on to have other children, or if your adopted child contacts you when he/she is an adult. Discuss the issues with your family, friends and a counsellor.

For expert advice, talk to your local council's adoption social worker or an adoption agency.

The adoption process

■ All adoption agencies offer counselling to help you understand your rights and responsibilities and the implications of what you're doing.

■ You may want to speak to a solicitor for legal advice.

■ The father may have to agree to the adoption. Speak to him as soon as you can, and be prepared to explain the reasons for your decision.

■ If you go ahead, the adoption agency will ask questions about your background and family's medical history.

■ Next, there are two alternatives: you can wait until the adoption agency has found the right family, then an adoption order transfers your legal rights (as a parent) to the adopters; or you can transfer your parental rights to the adoption agency (which are then transferred to the adoptive family). If a family hasn't been found after a year (and you've changed your mind), you can apply to become the child's legal parent again.

■ In both cases, a social worker will interview you. Then a signed agreement goes to the court for the adoption hearing. You can withdraw this agreement before the hearing, but you must tell the court immediately, and they may not rule in your favour.

■ When an adoption order is issued, all identities are confidential. However, agencies encourage direct or indirect contact if it's in the child's interest. You may be able to send cards and letters or speak on the phone.

■ If not, when the child is 18, he/she can apply for a birth certificate and leave a letter with the adoption agency. If you contact the agency, you will be able to get in touch.

Final word

Adolescence isn't all hormones and heartache but it's accepted that being a teenager in the twenty-first century is not easy. Finding out where you fit in the adult world is a natural process that brings its own stresses.

Being a teenager is about experimenting and pushing boundaries – which you can do in a safe, healthy and positive way. Making mistakes is part of growing up and if you admit your mistakes, you'll learn from them. Even the most cringe-making experience can be turned into a positive one if you learn what *not* to do.

Sometimes it's difficult to know who you are or what you think, so many changes are happening. It's easy to be swayed by other teenagers and it's easy to blend in when you're feeling un-confident or down, but if you have values, start living by them. You're an individual with individual needs, desires, likes, dislikes and principles.

Neither sex nor relationships go well if you don't feel right about what you're doing, or who you're doing it with. If you've read parts of this book you'll know that acting like an adult in sexual relationships isn't only about knowing your body, it's about knowing your mind.

Being ready for sex doesn't just happen as soon as you get an erection or start your periods. When you're ready for sex and a mature sexual relationship, you're prepared practically, intellectually and emotionally.

If you're out of control or confused there are people who can help and advise you. Don't ever feel alone with a problem – look around for role models to talk to or see Helpful Organisations in this book for contact details of knowledgeable people you can trust.

This book on Sex and Relationships is part of a series helping people like you overcome some of the difficulties of growing up and getting on. If there are other issues you'd like to get sorted, ask your Connexions Adviser for the Real Life Issues books on: Addictions, Bullying, Confidence and Self-Esteem, Coping with Life, Eating Disorders, Money, and Stress.

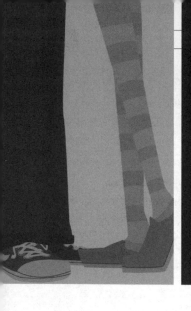

HELPFUL ORGANISATIONS

CHAPTER 1 FEELINGS

ChildLine
Freephone: 0800 1111
www.childline.org.uk
ChildLine is a free confidential helpline for any child or young person in trouble or in danger.

Eddie Surman Trust
359 Southwyck House
Clarewood Walk
London SW9 8TT
Tel: 020 7738 6893
Fax: 020 7733 8422
www.eddiesurmantrust.org.uk
For those feeling suicidal, have experienced the suicide of someone close, or with suicidal family or partners.

Relate Counselling Service for Young People
Tel: 0845 456 1310 (Ring for your nearest counselling service.)
www.relate.org.uk

www.ruok.net
Website of Wakefield and District Child and Adolescent Mental Health
Service (also known as CAMHS). Provides information on depression,
stress, self-harm, bullying and divorce for young people.

Samaritans
Tel: 08457 909090 (UK); 1850 609090 (ROI)
Email: jo@samaritans.org
www.samaritans.org.uk
Confidential listening service staffed all day, every day of the year, for
anyone troubled, despairing or suicidal.

Young Minds
Email: info@youngminds.org.uk
www.youngminds.org.uk
A mental health charity for children and young people, offering advice
for troubled teenagers and parents.

Youth Access (National Association of Young People's Advisory and
Counselling Services)
Tel: 020 8772 9900 (Ring for the nearest confidential young people's
counselling service.)

CHAPTER 2 FAMILIES

Relate Family Counselling Service
Tel: 0845 456 1310 (Ring for your nearest Family Counselling
Service.)
www.relate.org.uk

Divorce
www.itsnotyourfault.org
Website supported by NCH children's charity (www.nch.org.uk).

Step families
www.childline.org.uk/stepfamilies.asp

CHAPTER 3 FRIENDS
www.antibullying.net
Website supported by the Scottish Executive providing information for children and parents on bullying.

www.bullying.co.uk
The Bullying Online charity provides up-dated information on bullying for children and parents.

Kidscape
2 Grosvenor Gardens
London SW1W 0DH
Tel: 020 7730 3300; Helpline: 08451 205 204
Fax: 020 7730 7081
Email: webinfo@kidscape.org.uk
www.kidscape.org.uk
The bullying and abuse charity offers help and information for children, parents and professionals through its counsellors and website.

CHAPTER 4 JUST GOOD FRIENDS?
Flirting
Men Are from Mars, Women Are from Venus: A practical guide for improving communication and getting what you want in your relationships, John Gray, HarperCollins

Superflirt, Tracey Cox, Dorling Kindersley

Sexuality

www.avert.org

Black Lesbian and Gay Helpline
Tel: 020 8693 0520 (Sat from 11pm)

www.gayyouthuk.co.uk

London Lesbian and Gay Switchboard
Tel: 020 7837 7324
www.llgs.org.uk
For information and advice on being gay, lesbian or bisexual.

Naz Project London
Palingswick House
241 King Street
London W6 9LP
Tel: 020 8741 1879
Fax: 020 8741 9609
Email: npl@naz.org.uk
www.naz.org.uk
Support and advice for gay men and those with HIV/AIDS from South
Asian, Middle Eastern, North African, Horn of African and Latin
American communities.

Proud Start
Tel: 01452 30680
www.proudstart.org.uk
A group for gay people 14–21 years old coming to terms with their
sexuality. Meetings are held in Cheltenham on Wednesdays from
7.30pm.

CHAPTER 5 ROMANTIC RELATIONSHIPS
Relationships and marriage
Relate
Tel: 0845 130 4010 (Mon–Fri 9.30am–4.30pm)
www.relate.org.uk
Counselling for couples to help make sure your marriage gets off to the best possible start.

CHAPTER 6 LOVERS
www.bbc.co.uk/teens/

Relate sex therapy
0845 456 1310 (Ring for the nearest Sex Therapy Counselling Service.)
www.relate.org.uk
Relate provides counselling or sex therapy for people with sexual difficulties.

www.ruthinking.co.uk
Freephone: 0800 282930
A free confidential telephone helpline for under-18s. It's open from 7am to midnight to answer questions about sex and relationships.

SPOD (Association to Aid the Sexual and Personal Relationships of People with a Disability)
286 Camden Road
London N7 0BJ
Tel: 020 7607 8851
Fax: 020 7700 0236
Information and counselling for disabled people having sexual or relationship difficulties.

Sexual abuse

NCH

85 Highbury Park

London N5 1UD

Helpline: 0845 7 626 579 (lo-call number) (Mon–Fri 9am–5pm)

www.nch.org.uk

The Children's Charity helping young people affected by poverty, disability and abuse.

National Child Protection Helpline

Helpline: 0800 800 50; Minicom: 0800 056 0566

It offers counselling, information and advice for children and those concerned about a child at risk of abuse.

National Society for the Prevention of Cruelty to Children (NSPCC)

NSPCC National Centre

42 Curtain Road

London EC2A 3NH

Tel: 020 7825 2500; Helpline: 0808 800 5000

Fax: 020 7825 2525

Email: helpline@nspcc.org.uk

www.nspcc.org.uk

The NSPCC runs more than 80 child protection projects in England, Wales and Northern Ireland responding to the local needs of children and families. Private, confidential sessions are available.

There4me

www.there4me.com/home/index.asp

A website for all 12–16-year-olds living in the British Isles.

Sexual assault

Rape Crisis UK and Ireland

Truth About Rape

c/o CER

The Pankhurst Centre

Department 5

60-62 Nelson Street

Manchester M13 9WP

Tel: 0115 900 3560

www.rapecrisis.org.uk and www.truthaboutrape.co.uk

A website maintained by Truth About Rape for girls and women who have been raped or indecently assaulted. Local rape helpline numbers appear on the website.

Survivors UK

PO Box 2470

London SW9 6WQ

Tel: 0845 122 1201 (Tue and Thu 7pm–10pm)

Email: info@survivorsuk.org.uk

www.survivorsuk.co.uk

For boys and men who have been raped or indecently assaulted.

The Sex Book, Jane Pavanel, Wizard Books, 2003

A no-nonsense guide for teenagers.

CHAPTER 7 SEXPERTS
Contraception

Brook Advisory Centres

Freephone: 0800 018 5023

E-mail: information@brookcentres.org.uk

www.brook.org.uk

Provides free confidential sex advice for young people.

Brook also provides 24-hour recorded information on:

Emergency contraception: 020 7617 0801

Missed a period? 020 7617 0802

Sexually transmitted infections: 020 7617 0807

Starting contraception: 020 7617 0804

Visiting a Brook Centre: 020 7617 0806

Contraceptive Education Service

Tel: 020 7837 4044 (Mon–Fri 9am–7pm)

Helpline to answer enquiries on contraceptive use. Advises on sexual matters, including contraception, abortion and sexual health, will give details of local clinics. Single copies of leaflets on all methods of contraception are free with an SAE.

fpa (formerly The Family Planning Association)

2–12 Pentonville Road

London N1 9FP

Tel: 020 7837 4044

Helplines: England: 0845 310 1334 (Mon–Fri 9am–7pm); Scotland: 0141 576 5088 (Mon–Thu 9am–5pm, Fri 9am–4.30pm); Northern Ireland: 02890 325488 (Mon–Thu 9am–5pm, Fri 9am–4.30pm)

Fax: 020 7837 3042

www.fpa.org.uk

The fpa is a charity working to improve the sexual health and reproductive rights of all people throughout the UK. It provides information on all aspects of contraception, family planning services, and sexual health.

NetDoctor

Website:

www.netdoctor.co.uk/sex_relationships/facts/contraception_which.htm

Independent health website giving information on contraception.

Emergency contraception

www.levonelle.co.uk

Morning After Pill website with information on emergency contraception.

STIs

www.mindbodysoul.gov.uk

Health information for 14–16-year-olds

National AIDS Helpline

Freephone: 0800 567123

24-hour helpline offering confidential information and referrals on any aspect of HIV/AIDS.

Sexual Health Line

Tel: 0800 567123

www.playingsafely.co.uk

24-hour free confidential advice on STIs from the NHS.

HIV/AIDS

AVERT

4 Brighton Road

Horsham

West Sussex RH13 5BA

www.avert.org

Avert is an international HIV/AIDS charity based in England. The website provides information for young people (gay and straight) on HIV/AIDS and STIs.

Eddie Surman Trust (see above)
Positiveline: 0800 1696806 (Mon–Fri 11am–10pm, Sat–Sun 4pm–10pm)
Advice and support for anyone diagnosed HIV +.

National AIDS helpline
Freephone: 0800 567 123
24-hour helpline offering confidential information and referrals on HIV/AIDS.

CHAPTER 8 PREGNANCY

British Pregnancy Advisory Service (BPAS)
Austy Manor
Wootton Wawen
Solihull B95 6BX
Tel: 08457 304030 (Mon–Fri 8am–9pm, Sat 8.30am–6pm, Sun 9.30am–2.30pm)
www.bpas.org
Provides affordable contraception and abortion services. Offers pregnancy testing, crisis pregnancy counselling, abortion care, after-abortion support, sterilisation and vasectomy and emergency contraception. Website contains information for women thinking about an abortion, emergency contraception, pregnancy testing and what to do next.

Brook Advisory Centres
24-hour recorded information lines:
Abortion: 020 7617 0803

Pregnant and unsure? 020 7617 0805
E-mail: information@brookcentres.org.uk
www.brook.org.uk

www.ivillage.co.uk/pregnancyandbaby/
Website for women with advice for teenage and single parents.

www.maternityalliance.gov.uk
Website with advice on benefits and maternity rights.

Single Parents' Action Network
Tel: 0117 951 4231
A multi-racial organisation run by single parents working to improve
conditions for one-parent families.

Adoption

Department of Health
www.doh.gov.uk/adoption
The Government's official adoption site.

National Organisation for Counselling Adoptees and Their Parents
(NORCAP)
112 Church Road
Wheatley
Oxfordshire OX33 1LU
Tel: 01865 875 000 (Mon–Fri 10am–4pm)
Email: enquiries@norcap.org
www.norcap.org.uk
Can help you find your adopted child, should you wish to get in touch
in future.

Post-Adoption Centre
5 Torriano Mews
Torriano Avenue
London NW5 2RZ
Helpline: 020 7284 0555 (Mon–Wed and Fri 10am–1pm; Thu
5.30pm–7.30pm)
Email: advice@postadoptioncentre.org.uk
www.postadoptioncentre.org.uk
Provides counselling and a weekly drop-in for birth mothers to discuss
how adoption has affected their lives (London, Wed 2pm–3pm).

GENERAL INFORMATION

4 Nations Child Policy Network – England
8 Wakley Street
London EC1V 7QE
Tel: 020 7843 6068
Fax: 020 7843 6063
Email: info@childpolicy.org.uk
www.childpolicy.org.uk/
Information about policy, consultations and legislation relating to
children and young people.

Children's Legal Centre
University of Essex
Wivenhoe Park
Colchester CO4 3SQ
Tel: 01206 872466 (Helpline: 01206 873820, Mon–Fri
10am–12am and 2pm–5pm)
Fax: 01206 874026
Email: clc@essex.ac.uk
www.childrenslegalcentre.com/

A charity offering advice and support on legal matters, including exclusions, to young people, parents and guardians.

National Youth Agency
www.youthinformation.com
The National Youth Agency website gives information and advice on love and sex, law and justice, employment, and travel for young people.